NELSON'S
Little Books of
SERIES

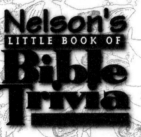

Nelson's
LITTLE BOOK OF
Bible
Trivia

NELSON'S
Little Books of
SERIES

# Nelson's
## LITTLE BOOK OF
# Bible Trivia

THOMAS NELSON PUBLISHERS
Nashville

The Publisher sincerely appreciates all those whose jokes or information are used in this book. We have made every effort to quote the source for each piece of information used. If we have inadvertently left anyone out, please let us know.

Special thanks to Allen Peabody for his contribition to the humor in this book.

Printed in Nashville, Tennessee, by Thomas Nelson, Inc.

Unless otherwise indicated, all Scripture quotations are from the New King James Version, copyright © 1979, 1980, 1982 by Thomas Nelson, Inc.

ISBN 0-7852-4707-6

Printed in the United States of America

2 3 4 5 — 05 04 03 02 01

# Table of Contents

# **Foreword**

The Bible is full of fascinating information. We have discovered this as we have pored over the many questions and answers that make up this book! We take the Bible very seriously, as the inspired Word of God, and have worked very hard to ensure that this book is as accurate as possible. All references are to the New King James Version of the Bible; each question and answer has been examined to make sure the interpretation is accurate and treated with the utmost respect.

Be intrigued with the information you will discover! Not only do you hold in your hands a thousand questions about the Bible and other topics that relate to it, but you are given bits of information in the "How About That!" sections that will add to your knowledge about the Bible and the times in which it was written. We find these bits of information especially helpful, as they aid in placing the events of the Bible alongside those of secular history.

As you go through this book, you will no doubt be surprised, shocked, and even humored by the facts you will uncover. Laugh! Enjoy the Scripture that God has given us! Nurture your sense of humor. Remember: Solomon, renowned for his wisdom, said, "There is . . . a time to laugh!" (Ecclesiastes 3:4)

Finally, let us encourage one another with the knowledge and experience that studying the Bible develops in us. It is full of practical ideas for happiness and purpose in this life, as well as promises for the life eternal. Share it with friends and family. We hope to help add some curiosity to your study of the Bible through your enjoyment of *Nelson's Little Book of Bible Trivia!*

# An Angel Gets Its Wings

## MULTIPLE CHOICE

1. **When he cloaked Himself as an angel, God appeared to whom by the spring on the way to Shur?**
   **A.** Hagar
   **B.** Abraham
   **C.** a leprechaun
   **D.** Sarah

2. **Who appeared to Moses in the burning bush, according to Exodus 3:2?**
   **A.** God
   **B.** Yahweh
   **C.** the Angel of the Lord
   **D.** The Lord of Hosts

3. **How did the Angel of the Lord address Gideon?**
   **A.** Gideon, the little wimp!
   **B.** Gideon, man of God
   **C.** Gideon, mighty warrior
   **D.** mighty man of valor

4. **Why did the Angel of the Lord call out, "Abraham, Abraham!"**
   **A.** so that he would turn and flee from danger
   **B.** so that he would not sacrifice his son Isaac
   **C.** because he was about to trip and fall into the animal's feeding trough, and he wanted to warn him

**D.** so that he would repent from his sin and turn to God

5. **What animal did an angel appear to?**
   **A.** Balaam's donkey
   **B.** Cleopatra's cat
   **C.** Jonah's whale
   **D.** Samson's lion

ANSWERS
p. 18

---

# HOW ABOUT THAT!

Angels are most often depicted as women (Matt 22:30) yet when they appear in the Bible as humans they are described as men (Gen 18, 19; Judg 13, Matt 28, Luke 24).

---

6. **The Angel of the Lord declared God's covenant of protection with Israel void at Bochim because of Israel's sin in:**
   **A.** not obeying God
   **B.** not sacrificing all the loot they recovered on their raids
   **C.** the Watergate scandal
   **D.** creating idols to worship instead of God

7. **Where did the Angel of the Lord sit when he appeared to Gideon?**

---

    **A.** on Gideon's cloak, in the cool of the day
    **B.** on a nettle
    **C.** under the terebinth tree which belonged to Gideon's father
    **D.** on the roof of Gideon's home

8. **What did the Angel of the Lord say to Manoah's wife?**
    **A.** she would give birth to Samuel
    **B.** she would give birth to Isaiah
    **C.** she would give birth to a submarine sandwich
    **D.** she would give birth to Samson

## FILL IN THE BLANKS

1. David saw an Angel of the Lord on the threshing floor _____ his people.

2. The Angel of the Lord commanded that David _____ _____ _____ on the _____ _____ of Ornan the Jebusite.

3. The Angel of the Lord provided _____ _____ _____ _____ _____ _____ __ _____ _____ for Elijah to eat on his journey to Horeb.

4. The Angel of the Lord protected Elijah from _____ _____ _____ by sending fire from

Heaven on them, after Elijah prophesied Ahaziah's death.

5. Sennacherib's Assyrian army was defeated when the _____ ___ _____ _____ killed _____ _____ in their sleep.

6. The Angel of the Lord _____ ___ _____ to Zechariah, telling him to _____ _____ _____ _____ _____ _____.

7. In Zechariah's vision of the High Priest, _____ _____ _____ stood before the Angel of the Lord and _____ stood at his right hand to oppose him.

ANSWERS
p. 18

## WORD BANK

a cake baked on coals and a jar of water

the high priest    striking    Satan

King Ahaziah's army    threshing floor

proclaim the word of the Lord

build an altar    explained a vision

185,000 soldiers    angel of the Lord

## MATCHING

| Quality of the Angel | Scripture Reference |
|---|---|

**1.** Created Being

a. "Are they not all ministering spirits sent forth to minister for those who will inherit salvation?"

**2.** God's Servant

b. "Suddenly, a hand touched me, which made me tremble on my knees and on the palms of my hands."

**3.** Invisible

c. ". . . nor can they die anymore, for they are equal to the angels and are sons of God, being sons of the resurrection."

**4.** Limited Spatially

d. "Praise Him, all His angels . . . For He commanded and they were created."

**5.** Organized in Ranks

e. "For by him all things were created that are in heaven and that are on the earth, visible and invisible, whether thrones or dominions or principalities or powers."

**6.** Named

f. "Bless the Lord, you His angels, who excel in strength, who do His word, heeding the voice of His word."

## MATCHING—cont'd

### Quality of the Angel

### Scripture Reference

**7.** Unmarried

g. "For in the resurrection they neither marry nor are given in marriage, but are like angels of God in heaven."

**8.** Spirits

h. "Now in the sixth month the angel Gabriel was sent by God to a city of Galilee named Nazareth . . ."

**9.** Undying

ANSWERS p. 19

i. ". . . his face was like the appearance of lightning, his eyes like torches of fire, his arms and feet like burnished bronze in color, and the sound of his words like the voice of a multitude."

**10.** Blue, Smurfy

j. "La, la, la, la, la, la, la, la, la, la, la . . ."

### TALL TALE

One day a very _____ angel was fly-
ADJECTIVE

ing to _____ like she did every day. As she
PLACE

was going, she bumped into a _____
NOUN

_____

that was not in a very _____ mood. "_____," she said to
ADJECTIVE                                                    APOLOGY

the _____. "I didn't see you there!"
NOUN

But the _____ simply looked at her like she
NOUN

was a _____. The _____ an-
NOUN                          ADJECTIVE

gel _____. The _____
VERB (PAST TENSE)                          NOUN

had made her very _____. But
EMOTION

then, the _____ also began
NOUN

to _____! The two be-
VERB

came _____ friends. From that day for-
ADJECTIVE

ward, they went to _____ together every
PLACE

day, and they lived _____ ever after!
ADVERB

## MATCHING

1. Hagar

2. Lot's wife

a. Gabriel announced the birth of John the Baptist to him.

b. The Angel of the Lord announced an end to her barrenness and described the special nature of her son's ministry.

## MATCHING—cont'd

**3.** Wife for Isaac

    c. Angels led her and her family by the hand, away from their burning home.

**4.** Samson's mother

    d. Angels announced the birth of Jesus to them near Bethlehem.

**5.** Mary's betrothed

    e. The Angel of the Lord gave helpful instructions, announced her future descendants, and offered comfort.

**6.** Women at the empty tomb

    f. Gabriel told her that she would be the mother of the Messiah, even though she had never been with a man.

**7.** Elizabeth's husband

    g. An angel calmed his fears of his wife's infidelity and announced her role in history to him.

**8.** Mary

    h. An angel appeared to tell them that Jesus was alive.

**9.** Shepherds who came to see Mary and Jesus.

    i. An angel guided Abraham's servant to the right woman.

ANSWERS p. 19

1. What stood above the train of God's robe in Isaiah 6?

   _____

2. What did the seraphim look like? _____

   _____

3. What did the seraphim say to one another?

   _____

   _____

4. Who said "Holy, holy, holy, Lord God Almighty, Who was and is and is to come" in Revelation?

_____

5. What is the name of the angel who saves George Bailey's life? _____

## UNSCRAMBLE (the names for Satan)

1. Dabadon
2. Nolyopla
3. Ezebelubb
4. Liebla
5. Lived
6. Rangod
7. Neyem
8. Ficuler
9. Tanas
10. Petermt

ANSWERS p. 21

## TRUE OR FALSE

1. Angels sleep.

2. Angels are called "sons of God."

3. Satan is called the god of this age.

4. The angels will bring peace among men on earth when Christ returns.

5. God, Himself, will separate the wicked from among the just at the end of the age.

6. The angels will gather the elect from the four winds, from the farthest part of earth to the farthest part of heaven.

7. An angel will bind Satan with a chain for one thousand years.

8. Satan is called the angel of the bottomless pit.

9. Angel hair pasta is made from actual angel hair.

**10.** The elder, not the angel, held the golden censer at the altar.

**MULTIPLE CHOICE**

**1. Angels appeared to Abraham in the form of:**
   **A.** three men
   **B.** white birds
   **C.** W-4s
   **D.** a multitude of women

ANSWERS p. 22

**2. The angel who appeared as a "certain man" to Daniel wore what?**
   **A.** a turban
   **B.** sandals of sapphire
   **C.** linen
   **D.** a gold belt
   **E.** Adidas

**3. The angel-men who wore shining garments appeared to whom at the tomb?**
   **A.** Peter and Thomas
   **B.** the women who had followed Jesus from Galilee
   **C.** John and Peter
   **D.** Peter, Paul, and Mary

**4. How do the angels minister in Psalm 104?**
   **A.** with flames of fire
   **B.** with a spirit of justice

# Top Ten Ways the Angels Tried to Get Lot's Family to Leave Sodom and Gomorrah

10. Raised their taxes.

9. Threatened to take up an offering.

8. Left a trail of Reeses' Pieces.

7. Sent a steady stream of door-to-door salesmen to their house.

6. Convinced the neighbors to put giant satellite dishes in their front lawns.

5. Loaded his mailbox with junk mail.

4. "Rolled" his house every weekend.

3. Encouraged the neighbor kids to ride their bikes and skateboards through his well-kept yard.

2. They Sodom-ped on them.

1. Put his phone number on a telemarketing phone list.

**C.** with the Evangelism Explosion method

**D.** with a rod of discipline

**5. In Psalm 68, God describes his angels as twenty-thousand what?**

**A.** voices

**B.** stars

**C.** teeny-boppers

**D.** chariots

**6. When did an angel rescue Paul?**

**A.** when he had too much credit card debt

**B.** when he was in prison

**C.** when he walked on water

**D.** when a crowd began to stone him

**7. Angels do which of the following: (more than one answer)**

**A.** announce events

**B.** quilt

**C.** attend church

**D.** carry messages

**E.** interpret visions

**F.** appear in dreams

**G.** investigate and punish sin

---

Q. How do we know angels don't use razors?

A. Because of the Christmas song: "Hark the hairy angel sings!"

---

**H.** watch over saints

**I.** marry

8. **Which of the following people were guided by angels?**
   **A.** Hagar
   **B.** Rebekah
   **C.** Joseph
   **D.** Cornelius
   **E.** All of the above

# ANSWERS TO:
## AN ANGEL GETS ITS WINGS

## MULTIPLE CHOICE

| # ANSWER | REFERENCE |
|----------|-----------|
| 1. a | Genesis 16:7–13 |
| 2. c | Exodus 3:2 |
| 3. d | Judges 6:12 |
| 4. b | Genesis 22 |
| 5. a | Numbers 22 |
| 6. a | Judges 2 |
| 7. c | Judges 6 |
| 8. d | Judges 13 |

## FILL IN THE BLANKS

| # ANSWER | REFERENCE |
|----------|-----------|
| 1. striking | 2 Samuel 24 |
| 2. build an altar, threshing floor | 1 Chronicles 21 |
| 3. a cake baked on coals and a jar of water | 1 Kings 19 |
| 4. King Ahaziah's army | 2 Kings 1 |
| 5. angel of the Lord, 185,000 soldiers | 2 Kings 19:35 |

| # ANSWER | REFERENCE |
|---|---|
| 6. explained a vision, proclaim the word of the Lord | Zechariah 1 |
| 7. the high priest, Satan | Zechariah 3 |

## MATCHING

| # ANSWER | REFERENCE |
|---|---|
| 1. d | Psalm 148:1–5 |
| 2. f | Psalm 103:19–21 |
| 3. e | Colossians 1:16 |
| 4. b | Daniel 10:10–20 |
| 5. i | Daniel 10:6 |
| 6. h | Luke 1:26 |
| 7. g | Matthew 22:30 |
| 8. a | Hebrews 1:14 |
| 9. c | Luke 20:36 |
| 10. j | |

## MATCHING

| # ANSWER | REFERENCE |
|---|---|
| 1. e | Genesis 16:7–12 |
| 2. c | Genesis 19 |
| 3. i | Genesis 24:1–7 |

## MATCHING—cont'd

| # ANSWER | REFERENCE |
|----------|-----------|
| 4. b | Judges 13:1–24 |
| 5. g | Matthew 1:20–25 |
| 6. h | Matthew 28:2–6 |
| 7. a | Luke 1:5–25 |
| 8. f | Luke 1:26–38 |
| 9. d | Luke 2:8–15 |

## SHORT ANSWER

| # ANSWER | REFERENCE |
|----------|-----------|
| 1. Seraphim | Isaiah 6:1–2 |
| 2. Each one had six wings: two covered its face, two covered its feet, and with two it flew. | Isaiah 6:2 |
| 3. "Holy, holy, holy is the Lord of hosts; The whole earth is full of His glory!" | Isaiah 6:3 |
| 4. The four living creatures, each having six wings, were full of eyes around and within. | Revelation 4:8 |
| 5. Clarence | |

## UNSCRAMBLE

| # ANSWER | REFERENCE |
| --- | --- |
| 1. Abaddon | Revelation 9:11 |
| 2. Apollyon | Revelation 9:11 |
| 3. Beelzebub | Matthew 12:24 |
| 4. Belial | 2 Corinthians 6:15 |
| 5. Devil | John 8:44 |
| 6. Dragon | Revelation 12:7 |
| 7. Enemy | Matthew 13:39 |
| 8. Lucifer | Isaiah 14:12–21 |
| 9. Satan | Mark 1:12–13 |
| 10. Tempter | 1 Thessalonians 3:5 |

## TRUE OR FALSE

| # ANSWER | REFERENCE |
| --- | --- |
| 1. False; do not sleep | Revelation 4:8 |
| 2. True | Job 2:1 |
| 3. True | 2 Corinthians 4:4 |
| 4. False; God will give peace | 2 Thessalonians 1:7 |
| 5. False; the angel will separate | Matthew 13:49 |
| 6. True | Mark 13:27 |
| 7. True | Revelation 20:1–3 |
| 8. True | Revelation 9:11 |
| 9. False | |
| 10. False; the angel held the golden censer | Revelation 8:3 |

## MULTIPLE CHOICE

| # | ANSWER | REFERENCE |
|---|--------|-----------|
| 1. | a | Genesis 18 |
| 2. | c,d | Daniel 10 |
| 3. | b | Luke 24 |
| 4. | a | Psalm 104 |
| 5. | d | Psalm 68:17 |
| 6. | b | Acts 12 |
| 7. | a,d,e,f,h | Genesis 16, 24; Judges 13, Matthew 1:20, Acts 10:3 |
| 8. | e | Acts 10:7 |

**Q.** What do angels and Martha Stewart have in common?

**A.** They are both heavenly hosts!

# Bible
# Translations

1. **The word "Bible" literally means:**
   A. the books
   B. the words of God
   C. many words, small print
   D. holy words

2. **Which religion(s) considers the Old Testament to be Scripture?**
   A. Christianity
   B. Islam
   C. Buddhism
   D. Judaism

ANSWERS
p. 39

3. **In the 18th and 19th centuries, and following, the divine inspiration of Scripture was:**
   A. rejected
   B. questioned
   C. undoubtedly accepted
   D. on vacation in the Caribbean

4. **Pope Leo XIII called the sacred writers:**
   A. infallible geniuses
   B. boy wonders
   C. progenitors of God's will
   D. instruments of the Holy Spirit

5. **Which word, meaning "a measuring rod, or a law," is the term used to describe the body of Scripture?**

**A.** canon
**B.** rifle
**C.** Torah
**D.** Septuagint

6. **Martin Luther suggested that which book be removed from the canon?**
   **A.** Leviticus
   **B.** Gone with the Wind
   **C.** The Gospel of Matthew
   **D.** The Epistle of James

7. **Which is NOT one of the three parts of the Hebrew Scriptures:**

**A.** Law
**B.** Poetry
**C.** Prophets
**D.** Writings

8. **Which of Josephus' rules for the Old Testament canon is incorrect:**
   **A.** the fixed number of books
   **B.** that they are sacred
   **C.** their divine origin
   **D.** that they were written between the time of Moses and Artaxerxes I

**TRUE OR FALSE**

1. Catholics and Protestants agree on which books should be included in the Bible.

2. The section of the Hebrew Old Testament called "Law" is also known as "The Pentatuch."

3. "The Prophets" is the section of the Bible that Protestants know as the books of Isaiah through Malachi.

4. In 200 B.C. major religious leaders gathered together and closed the Old Testament canon.

5. The B-I-B-L-E, that's the book for me!

ANSWERS
p. 39

6. The apocrypha is the religious books not included in the Protestant canon of Scripture.

7. Most of the Old Testament was written in Hebrew, but parts were written in Aramaic and parts in Greek.

8. All of the New Testament was composed in Greek.

9. The first Old Testament book to be printed was Genesis in Bologna, A.D. 1477.

10. The Dead Sea Scrolls were discovered in caves near the ancient community of Qumran.

## FILL IN THE BLANKS

1. The original manuscripts of the New Testament books are called _____.

2. God promised to _____ His Word.

3. _____ copied the manuscripts by _____.

4. Autographs were written in _____ Greek.

# Top Ten Failed Bible Translations

10. Latin Vulgar

9. Revised Unauthorized Version

8. American Slandered Version

7. King Tut Version

6. New Irrational Version

5. New Umbilical Version

4. Fill-in-the-Blank Bible

3. Pig Latin Vulgate

2. The Bible According to Disney

1. Prehistoric Moments Bible

**5.** _____ _____ is the process of comparing different manuscripts.

**6.** _____ printed the first Greek New Testament in _____.

**7.** Erasmus' text was revised and improved and called the _____ _____.

**8.** The _____ _____ was compiled from manuscripts Erasmus found in _____, _____.

ANSWERS p. 40

## WORD BANK

modern     Textual criticism     digest

Reykjavik, Iceland     Fashion integration

hand     folds     koine

Erasmus, 1516     autographs     preserve

Elves     Nouveau Version

Scribes     crayon     Textus Receptus

Raphael, 1731     Basel, Switzerland

## SHORT ANSWER

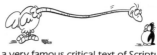

1. Who produced a very famous critical text of Scripture in A.D. 1882? _____

2. What method did Westcott and Hort use in producing their text? _____

_____

_____

_____

3. What contribution did J. J. Wettstein make to the printing of the New Testament? _____

_____

_____

4. The translation of the Hebrew Scriptures into Greek in the 3rd century B.C. is known as what?

_____

5. The legend surrounding the Septuagint says that this number of translators were sent from Jerusalem to Alexandria. _____

6. St. Jerome's translation of the Scriptures into Latin was called what? _____

**7.** The Vulgate was printed in A.D. 1455 by whom? _____

**8.** The first Catholic Bible to be printed in the United States of America was printed in A.D. 1790 in what city? _____

---

# HOW ABOUT THAT!

Martin Luther suggested that the book of James, among others, shouldn't be included in the Bible because of its emphasis on good works!

---

**PUT THE FOLLOWING IN ORDER (from earliest to latest)**

1. Tyndale Bible
2. New International Version
3. King James Version
4. Revised Version
5. Geneva Bible
6. New King James Version
7. American Standard Version

ANSWERS
p. 41

---

1. **The word "Apocrypha" means:**
   **A.** myth
   **B.** false
   **C.** hidden
   **D.** special

2. **What is a codex?**
   **A.** collection of books
   **B.** handwritten manuscript in book form
   **C.** set of letters
   **D.** printed copies of manuscripts

ANSWERS p. 42

3. **The exegeses of the Bible by the rabbis in the second century is:**
   **A.** Midrashim
   **B.** Pescherim
   **C.** allegories
   **D.** stories

4. **What book is not in the General Epistles?**
   **A.** James
   **B.** Revelation
   **C.** Romans
   **D.** 1 John

5. **Which of the following is considered extra-canonical?**

**A.** Gospel of Peter
**B.** 1 Peter
**C.** 2 Peter
**D.** Mark

6. _____ emphasized allegorical interpretation combining Greek thought with Jewish religion.
   **A.** Josephus
   **B.** Esdras
   **C.** Hezekiah
   **D.** Philo

7. _____ published a Greek New Testament in 1516 and dedicated it to Pope Leo X.
   **A.** Luther
   **B.** Erasmus

**C.** Calvin

**D.** Ignatius Loyola

8. **On which book did John Calvin *not* write a commentary?**
   **A.** Galatians
   **B.** John
   **C.** Romans
   **D.** Revelation

## MATCHING

| **Bible Version** | **Version It Is Based on or Translators** |
|---|---|
| 1. King James Version | a. Catholic Bible Association of America |
| 2. Revised Authorized Version | b. American Standard Version |
| 3. Revised Standard Version | c. Revised Standard Version |
| 4. New English Bible | d. Bishop's Bible |
| 5. Revised Version | e. King James Version |
| 6. New American Bible | f. New King James Version |
| 7. Jerusalem Bible | g. New York Bible Society |

ANSWERS p. 42

| Bible Version | Version It Is Based on or Translators |
|---|---|
| 8. American Standard Version | h. La Bible de Jérusalem and Vulgate |
| 9. New International Version | i. Revised Version |
| 10. New Revised Standard Version | j. original languages only |

## FILL IN THE BLANKS

1. The _____ Bible was under censure during the Reformation and, therefore, was not _____.

2. _____ _____ translated the New Testament into German in 1522.

3. The Authorized Version, or _____ _____ _____, used much of _____'s translation without changing it.

4. In 1534, _____ was petitioned by the Canterbury Convocation to have the whole Bible translated into _____.

**5.** _____ _____, probably

not knowing the _____ language,

translated a Bible into English from German and ded-

icated it to the _____ of

_____ in 1535.

ANSWERS
p. 43

---

# HOW ABOUT THAT!

The Printer's Bible, an early English translation, contains an ironic typo—''Printers have persecuted me without a cause.'' (Ps. 119:161)

---

**6.** The 1537 _____ _____

was the first Bible to receive the King's authorization.

**7.** Cromwell sponsored the printing of The _____

Bible in Paris in 1539.

**8.** The Geneva Bible became popular in England under

the rule of _____ _____.

---

## WORD BANK

Hebrew      Queen Elizabeth I

Matthew Bible      Martin Luther      Wycliff

Great      Henry VIII

King James Version      English

printed      Miles Coverdale      King

England      Tyndale

### UNSCRAMBLE (the Bible translations)

1. Wne Tinarlonetian Sevrnio

2. Wen Rasujemle Libeb

3. Hutridoaze Risoven

4. Nigvil Bleib

5. Dogo Wesn Liebb

6. Nestiwretsm Sonevri fo het Lohy Pitresucrs

7. Viresde Danstrad Sivoner

8. Siprocue Temonsm Libeb

9. Lavugte Libbe

10. Dacoevrel's Elbib

ANSWERS
p. 43

# ANSWERS TO:
# BIBLE TRANSLATIONS

From http://www.pilgrimworks.com/trans.htm

The New Catholic Encyclopedia. Catholic UP: Washington, D.C., 1967.

The Oxford Dictionary of the Christian Church. Cross, F. L., ed. Oxford UP: Oxford, 1997.

## MULTIPLE CHOICE

| # | ANSWER |
|---|--------|
| 1. | a |
| 2. | c |
| 3. | b |
| 4. | d |
| 5. | a |
| 6. | d |
| 7. | b |
| 8. | d |

## TRUE OR FALSE

| # | ANSWER |
|---|--------|
| 1. | False; Protestants exclude the Apocrypha |
| 2. | True |

## TRUE OR FALSE—cont'd

| # | ANSWER |
|---|--------|
| 3. | False (also includes Joshua through Kings) |
| 4. | False (The meeting to close the Old Testament canon was not held in 200 B.C..) |
| 5. | Up to you! |
| 6. | True |
| 7. | True |
| 8. | True |
| 9. | False (Psalms) |
| 10. | True |

## FILL IN THE BLANKS

| # | ANSWER |
|---|--------|
| 1. | autographs |
| 2. | preserve |
| 3. | Scribes, hand |
| 4. | koine |
| 5. | Textual criticism |
| 6. | Erasmus, 1516 |
| 7. | Textus Receptus |
| 8. | Textus Receptus, Basel, Switzerland |

## SHORT ANSWER

| # | ANSWER |
|---|--------|
| 1. | Westcott and Hort |
| 2. | verse-by-verse comparison |
| 3. | capital letters |
| 4. | the Septuagint |
| 5. | 72, thus the "septuagint" |
| 6. | the Vulgate |
| 7. | Johann Gutenberg |
| 8. | Philadelphia |

## PUT THE FOLLOWING IN ORDER

| # | ANSWER |
|---|--------|
| 1. | Tyndale Bible (1525) |
| 2. | Geneva Bible (1557) |
| 3. | King James Version (1611) |
| 4. | Revised Version (1881) |
| 5. | American Standard Version (1901) |
| 6. | New International Version (1973) |
| 7. | New King James Version (1982) |

## MULTIPLE CHOICE

| # | ANSWER |
|---|--------|
| 1. | c |
| 2. | b |
| 3. | a |
| 4. | c |
| 5. | a |
| 6. | d |
| 7. | b |
| 8. | d |

## MATCHING

| # | ANSWER |
|---|--------|
| 1. | d |
| 2. | f |
| 3. | b |
| 4. | j |
| 5. | e |
| 6. | a |
| 7. | h |
| 8. | i |
| 9. | g |
| 10. | c |

## FILL IN THE BLANKS

| # | ANSWER |
|---|--------|
| 1. | Wycliff, printed |
| 2. | Martin Luther |
| 3. | King James Version, Tyndale |
| 4. | Henry VIII, English |
| 5. | Miles Coverdale, Hebrew, King, England |
| 6. | Matthew Bible |
| 7. | Great |
| 8. | Queen Elizabeth I |

## UNSCRAMBLE

| # | ANSWER |
|---|--------|
| 1. | New International Version |
| 2. | New Jerusalem Bible |
| 3. | Authorized Version |
| 4. | Living Bible |
| 5. | Good News Bible |
| 6. | Westminster Version of the Holy Scriptures |
| 7. | Revised Standard Version |

| # | ANSWER |
|---|---|

8. Precious Moments Bible

9. Vulgate Bible

10. Coverdale's Bible

Q. Why did St. Jerome buy a watch?

A. Because he was always translate!

# TEXT AND TRANSLATIONS

## ENGLISH VERSIONS

English readers have had access to many versions of the Bible in the past four centuries. This list gives the date, title, and translator of over 200 English versions of Scripture. It is based upon more extensive lists by John H. Skilton and A. S. Herbert. Where the translator's name is unknown, or where a group of translators contributed to a particular work, the version is identified by the publisher's name (shown in parentheses):

| DATE | VERSION | TRANSLATOR/ PUBLISHER |
|------|---------|------------------------|
| 1526 | (The New Testament: untitled) | William Tyndale |
| 1530 | The Psalter of David in Englishe | George Joye |
| 1530 | (The Pentatuch: untitled) | William Tyndale |
| 1531? | The Prophete Jonas | William Tyndale |
| 1534 | Jeremy the Prophete, translated into Englisshe | George Joye |
| 1534 | The New Testament | George Joye |
| 1535 | Biblia: The Byble | George Coverdale |
| 1536 | The Newe Testament yet once agayne corrected | William Tyndale |
| 1537? | (The New Testament) | Miles Coverdale |
| 1537 | The Byble | (Richard Grafton and Edward Whitchurch) |
| 1539 | The Most Sacred Bible (Taverner's Bible) | Richard Taverner |

| DATE | VERSION | TRANSLATOR/ PUBLISHER |
|------|---------|------------------------|
| 1539 | The Byble in Englyshe (The Great Bible) | (Richard Grafton and Edward Whitchurch) |
| 1539 | The newe Testament of oure sauyour Jesu Christ | Miles Coverdale |
| 1539 | The New Testament in Englysshe | Richard Taverner |
| 1539 | The new Testament in Englyshe | (Richard Grafton and Edward Whitchurch) |
| 1540 | The Byble in Englyshe | Miles Coverdale |
| 1548? | Certayne Psalmes chose out of the Psalter | Thomas Starnhold |
| 1549 | The first tome or volume of the Paraphrase of Erasmus vpon The newe Testament | (Edward Whitchurch) |
| 1557 | The Newe Testament of ovr Lord Jesus Christ | William Whittingham |
| 1560 | The Bible and Holy Scriptvres conteyned in the Olde and Newe Testament (The Geneva Bible) | William Whittingham |
| 1562 | The Whole Booke of Psalmes | Thomas Starnhold and I. Hopkins |
| 1568 | The holie Bible (The Bishops' Bible) | Matthew Parker |
| 1582 | The New Testament of Iesvs Christ (Rheims New Testament) | Gregory Martin |
| 1611 | The Holy Bible (The King James Version) | (Robert Barker) |
| 1612 | The Book of Psalmes | Henry Ainsworth |

| DATE | VERSION | TRANSLATOR/ PUBLISHER |
|------|---------|----------------------|
| 1657 | The Dutch Annotations upon the whole Bible | Theodore Haak |
| 1700 | The Psalmes of David | C. Caryll |
| 1726 | A new version of all the Books of the New Testament | (J. Batly and S. Chandler) |
| 1727 | The books of Job, Psalms, proverbs, Eccleseastes, and the Song of Solomon | (J. Walthoe) |
| 1731 | The New Testament . . . Translated out of the Latin Vulgate by John Wiclif . . . about 1378 | John Lewis |
| 1741 | A new version of St. Matthew's Gospel | Daniel Scott |
| 1745 | Mr. Whiston's Primitive New Testament | William Whiston |
| 1761 | Divers parts of the holy Scriptures | Mr. Mortimer |
| 1764 | All the books of the Old and New Testament | Anthony Purver |
| 1764 | The New Testament | Richard Wynne |
| 1765 | The Psalms of David | Christopher Smart |
| 1765 | The New Testament | Philip Doddridge |
| 1768 | A Liberal Translation of the New Testament | Edward Harwood |
| 1770 | The New Testament or New Covenant | John Worsley |
| 1771 | The Book of Job | Thomas Scott |
| 1773 | The Pentateuch of Moses and the Historical Books of the Old Testament | Julius Bate |
| 1779 | Isaiah | Robert Lowth |

| DATE | VERSION | TRANSLATOR/ PUBLISHER |
|------|---------|-----------------------|
| 1779 | Essay towards a literal English version of the New Testament, in the Epistle of the Apostle Paul directed to the Ephesians | John Callander |
| 1782 | The Gospel of St. Matthew | Gilbert Wakefield |
| 1784 | Jeremiah and Lamentations | Benjamin Blayney |
| 1787 | The First (-Fifth) Book of Moses | David Levi |
| 1787 | The Apostle Paul's First and Second Epistles to the Thessalonians | James MacKnight |
| 1789 | A new English Translation of the Pentateuch | Isaac Delgado |
| 1789 | The Four gospels | George Campbell |
| 1790 | The Book of Psalms | Stephen Street |
| 1791 | The New Testament | Gilbert Wakefield |
| 1795 | The New Testament | Thomas Haweis |
| 1796 | Jonah | George Benjoin |
| 1796 | An Attempt toward revising our English translation of the Greek Scriptures | William Newcome |
| 1797 | The Holy Bible | Alexander Geddes |
| 1799 | A Revised Translation and Interpretation of the Sacred Scriptures | David Macrae |
| 1805 | The Book of Job | Joseph Stock |
| 1807 | The Gothic Gospel of Saint Matthew | Samuel Henshall |
| 1808 | The Holy Bible | Charles Thomson |
| 1810 | The Book of Job | Elizabeth Smith |

| DATE | VERSION | TRANSLATOR/ PUBLISHER |
|------|---------|-----------------------|
| 1811 | Canticles: or Song of Solomon | John Fry |
| 1812 | The Book of Job | John Mason Good |
| 1812 | The New Testament | W. Williams |
| 1816 | The English Version of the Polyglott Bible | (Samuel Bagster) |
| 1819 | Lyra Davidis (Psalms) | John Fry |
| 1822 | The Epistles of Paul the Apostle | Thomas Belsham |
| 1825 | The Book of Job | George Hunt |
| 1825 | The Psalms | J. Parkhurst |
| 1827 | An Amended Version of the Book of Job | George R. Noyes |
| 1827 | Liber Ecclesiasticus, the Book of the Church | Luke Howard |
| 1828 | The Gospel of God's Anointed | Alexander Greaves |
| 1831 | The Book of Psalms | George R. Noyes |
| 1833 | A literal translation from the Hebrew of the twelve Minor Prophets | A. Pick |
| 1833 | A New and Corrected Version of the New Testament | Rodolphus Dickinson |
| 1834 | The Gospel according to Matthew | William J. Aislabie |
| 1835 | The Book of the Law from the Holy Bible (The Pentateuch) | Joseph Ablett |
| 1837 | A New Translation of the Hebrew Prophets | George R. Noyes |
| 1837 | The Gospel of John | William J. Aislabie |
| 1843 | The Gospel according to Saint Matthew, and part of the first chapter of the Gospel according to Saint Mark | Sir John Cheke |

| DATE | VERSION | TRANSLATOR/ PUBLISHER |
|------|---------|------------------------|
| 1843 | Horae aramaicae: comprising concise notices of the Aramean dialects in general and of the versions of the Holy Scripture extant in them: with a translation of Matthew | J. W. Etheridge |
| 1846 | The book of Psalms | John Jebb |
| 1846 | A New Translation of the Proverbs, Ecclesiastes and the Canticles | George R. Noyes |
| 1846 | The Four Gospels from the Peschito | J. W. Etheridge |
| 1848 | The New Testament | Jonathan Morgan |
| 1848 | St. Paul's Epistle to the Romans | Herman Heinfetter |
| 1849 | The Apostolic Acts and Epistles | J. W. Etheridge |
| 1850 | The Bible Revised | Francis Barham |
| 1851 | The New Testament | James Murdock |
| 1851 | The Epistle of Paul to the Romans | Joseph Turnbull |
| 1851 | The Epistles of Paul the apostle to the Hebrews | Herman Heinfetter |
| 1854 | The Epistles of Paul the Apostle | Joseph Turnbull |
| 1855 | The Book of Genesis | Henry E. J. Howard |
| 1855 | A Translation of the Gospels | Andrews Norton |
| 1857 | The Books of Exodus and Leviticus | Henry E. J. Howard |
| 1858 | The New Testament | Leicester A. Sawyer |
| 1859 | A Revised Translation of the New Testament | W. G. Cookesley |

| DATE | VERSION | TRANSLATOR/ PUBLISHER |
|---|---|---|
| 1860 | The Psalms | Lord Congleton |
| 1861 | Jewish School and Family Bible | A. Benisch |
| 1861? | The New Testament . . . As Revised and Corrected by the Spirits | Leonard Thorn |
| 1862 | The New Testament | H. Highton |
| 1863 | The Holy Bible | Robert Young |
| 1863 | The Psalms | W. Kay |
| 1863 | The Book of Daniel | John Bellamy |
| 1864 | The Book of Job | J. M. Rodwell |
| 1864 | The Emphatic Diaglott | Benjamin Wilson |
| 1867 | The Minor Prophets | John Bellamy |
| 1869 | The Book of Job in metre | William Meikle |
| 1869 | The Book of Psalms | Charles Carter |
| 1870 | The New Testament | John Bowes |
| 1871 | The Book of Job | Francis Barham |
| 1871 | The Book of Psalms | Francis Barham and Edward Hare |
| 1871 | St. John's Epistles | Francis Barham |
| 1871? | The Gospels, Acts, Epistles, and Book of Revelation | John Darby |
| 1876 | The Holy Bible | Julia E. Smith |
| 1877 | The New Testament | John Richter |
| 1877 | Revised English Bible | (Eyre and Spottis-woode) |
| 1881 | The New Testament: English Revised Version | (Kambridgel University Press) |
| 1882? | St. Paul's Epistle to the Romans | Ferrar Fenton |
| 1884 | The Psalter . . . and certain Canticles | Richard Rolle |

| DATE | VERSION | TRANSLATOR/ PUBLISHER |
|------|---------|-----------------------|
| 1884 | The Book of Psalms | T. K. Cheyne |
| 1884 | St. Paul's Epistles in Modern English | Ferrar Fenton |
| 1885 | The Old Testament Scriptures | Helen Spurrell |
| 1885 | The Holy Bible: Revised Version | (Oxford University Press) |
| 1894 | A Translation of the Four Gospels from the Syriac of the Sinaitic Palimpsest | Agnes S. Lewis |
| 1897 | The New Dispensation: The New Testament | Robert Weekes |
| 1898 | The Book of Job | Ferrar Fenton |
| 1898 | The Twentieth Century New Testament | (W. and J. Mackay and Co.) |
| 1898 | The Four Gospels | Seymour Spencer |
| 1899 | The Old and New Testament | (J. Clarke and Co.) |
| 1900 | St. Paul's Epistle to the Romans | W. G. Rutherford |
| 1901 | The Holy Bible: American Standard Version | (Thomas Nelson and Sons) |
| 1901 | The Five Books of Moses | Ferrar Fenton |
| 1901 | The Historical New Testament | James Moffatt |
| 1902? | The Bible in Modern English | Ferrar Fenton |
| 1903 | The Book of Psalms | Kaufman Kohler |
| 1903 | The New Testament in Modern Speech | Richard Weymouth |
| 1903 | The Revelation | Henry Forster |
| 1904 | The New Testament | Adolphus S. Worrell |
| 1906 | St. John's Gospel, Epistles, and Revelation | Henry Forster |
| 1908 | Thessalonians and Corinthians | W. G. Rutherford |

| DATE | VERSION | TRANSLATOR/ PUBLISHER |
|------|---------|------------------------|
| 1912 | The Book of Ruth | R.H.J. Steuart |
| 1913 | The New Testament | James Moffatt |
| 1914 | The Poem of Job | Edward King |
| 1916 | The Wisdom of Ben-Sira (Ecclesiasticus) | W.O.E. Oesterley |
| 1917 | The Holy Scriptures according to the Masoretic text | (The Jewish Publication Society of America) |
| 1918 | The New Testament (The Shorter Bible) | Charles Foster Kent |
| 1920? | Amos | Theodore H. Robinson |
| 1921 | The Old Testament (The Shorter Bible) | Charles Foster Kent |
| 1921 | Mark's Account of Jesus | T.W. Pym |
| 1923 | The New Testament. An American Translation | Edgar J. Goodspeed |
| 1923 | The Riverside New Testament | William G. Ballantine |
| 1924 | The Old Testament | James Moffatt |
| 1924 | Centenary Translation of the New Testament | Helen B. Montgomery |
| 1925 | Hebrews | F.H. Wales |
| 1927 | The Old Testament | J.M. Powis Smith, T.J. Meek, Alexander R. Gordon, Leroy Waterman |
| 1927 | St. Matthew's Gospel | (T. and T. Clark) |
| 1928 | The Psalms Complete | William W. Martin |
| 1928 | The Christian's Bible: New Testament | George LeFevre |

| DATE | VERSION | TRANSLATOR/ PUBLISHER |
|------|---------|----------------------|
| 1933 | The Four Gospels according to the Eastern Version | George M. Lamsa |
| 1933 | The Four Gospels | Charles C. Torrey |
| 1936 | The Song of Songs | W.O.E. Oesterley |
| 1937 | The Psalms and the Canticles of the Divine Office | George O'Neill |
| 1937 | The New Testament | Johannes Greber |
| 1937 | The New Testament | Charles B. Williams |
| 1937 | St. Paul from the Trenches | Gerald Cornish |
| 1938 | Job | George O'Neill |
| 1938 | The New Testament | Edgar L. Clementson |
| 1939 | Ecclesiasticus | A. D. Power |
| 1944 | The New Testament | Ronald A. Knox |
| 1945 | The Berkeley Version of the New Testament | Gerrit Verkuyl |
| 1946 | The Psalms . . . Also the Canticles of the Roman Breviary | (Benziger Bros.) |
| 1946 | The New Testament (Revised Standard Version) | (Thomas Nelson and Sons) |
| 1947 | The Psalms | Ronald A. Knox |
| 1947 | The New Testament | George Swann |
| 1947 | Letters to Young Churches: Epistles of the New Testament | J.B. Phillips |
| 1949 | The Old Testament | Ronald A. Knox |
| 1950 | The New Testament of Our Messiah and Saviour Yahshua | A.B. Traina |
| 1950 | New World Translation: New Testament | (Watchtower Bible and Tract Society) |
| 1952 | The Four Gospels | E.V. Rieu |

| DATE | VERSION | TRANSLATOR/ PUBLISHER |
|---|---|---|
| 1952 | The Holy Bible: Revised Standard Version | (Thomas Nelson and Sons) |
| 1954 | The New Testament | James A. Kliest and Joseph Lilly |
| 1954 | The Amplified Bible: Gospel of John | The Lockman Foundation |
| 1955 | The Authentic New Testament | Hugh J. Schonfield |
| 1956 | The Inspired Letters in Clearest English | Frank C. Laubach |
| 1957 | The Holy Bible from Ancient Eastern Manuscripts | George M. Lamsa |
| 1958 | The New Testament in Modern English | J.B. Phillips |
| 1958 | The Amplified Bible: New Testament | The Lockman Foundation |
| 1959 | The Holy Bible: The Berkeley Version in Modern English | (Zondervan Publishing Co.) |
| 1960 | The Holy Bible (New American Standard) | (Thomas Nelson and Sons) |
| 1960 | The New World Translation: Old Testament | (Watchtower Bible and Tract Society, Inc.) |
| 1961 | The New English Bible: New Testament | (Oxford University Press and Cambridge University Press) |
| 1962 | The Children's Version of the Holy Bible | J.P. Green |
| 1962 | Modern King James Version of the Holy Bible | (McGraw-Hill) |
| 1962 | Living Letters: The Paraphrased Epistles | Kenneth Taylor |

| DATE | VERSION | TRANSLATOR/ PUBLISHER |
|---|---|---|
| 1962 | The Amplified Bible: Old Testament Part II | The Lockman Foundation |
| 1962 | The New Jewish Version | Jewish Publication Society |
| 1963 | The New Testament in the Language of Today | William Beck |
| 1963 | The New American Standard Bible: New Testament | The Lockman Foundation |
| 1964 | The Amplified Bible: Old Testament Part I | The Lockman Foundation |
| 1966 | Good News for Modern Man: The New Testament | (American Bible Society) |
| 1966 | The Living Scriptures: A New Translation in the King James Tradition | (American Bible Society) |
| 1966 | The Jerusalem Bible | |
| 1968 | The Cotton Patch Version of Paul's Epistles | Clarence Jordan |
| 1968 | The New Testament of Our Master and Saviour | (Missionary Dispensary Bible Research) |
| 1969 | The New Testament: A New Translation | William Barclay |
| 1969 | Modern Language New Testament | (Zondervan Publishing Co.) |
| 1969 | The Cotton Patch Version of Luke and Acts | Clarence Jordan |
| 1970 | New American Bible | (St. Anthony Guild Press) |
| 1970 | New English Bible | (Oxford University Press and Cambridge University Press) |

| DATE | VERSION | TRANSLATOR/PUBLISHER |
|---|---|---|
| 1970 | The Cotton Patch Version of Matthew and John | Clarence Jordan |
| 1971 | Letters from Paul | Boyce Black-Welder |
| 1971 | New American Standard Bible | The Lockman Foundation |
| 1971 | King James II Version of the Bible | (Associated Publishers and Authors) |
| 1971 | The Living Bible | (Tyndale House) |
| 1972 | The New Testament in Modern English, Revised Edition | J.B. Phillips |
| 1973 | The New International Version: New Testament | (Zondervan Bible Publishers) |
| 1973 | The Translator's New Testament | (The British and Foreign Bible Society) |
| 1973 | The Cotton Patch Version of Hebrews and the General Epistles | Clarence Jordan |
| 1973 | The Poetic Bible | Veo Gray |
| 1976 | Good News Bible | (American Bible Society) |
| 1977 | The Holy Bible in the Language of Today | William Beck |
| 1978 | The New International Version | (Zondervan Bible Publishers) |
| 1979 | The New King James Version: New Testament | (Thomas Nelson Publishers) |
| 1982 | The Holy Bible, New King James Version | (Thomas Nelson Publishers) |
| 1986 | The New Jerusalem Bible | |
| 1989 | New Revised Standard Bible | (Thomas Nelson Publishers and others) |

| DATE | VERSION | TRANSLATOR/ PUBLISHER |
|------|---------|-----------------------|
| 1989 | Revised English Bible | (Oxford University Press and Cambridge University Press) |
| 1991 | Contemporary English Version, New Testament | (American Bible Society and Thomas Nelson Publishers) |
| 1995 | Contemporary English Version | (American Bible Society and Thomas Nelson Publishers) |
| 1996 | New Living Bible | (Tyndale Publishers) |

# Famous (and not-so-famous) Figures

1. **Who hovered over the surface of the waters during Creation?**
   A. arch-angels
   B. cherubim and seraphim
   C. the Spirit of God
   D. Adam and Eve

ANSWERS
p. 72

2. **Adam's name means:**
   A. man
   B. red
   C. first person
   D. mankind's sorrow

---

# HOW ABOUT THAT!

When King David was ruling Israel, the Chinese developed a textbook for Mathematics!

---

3. **Eve's name means:**
   A. mother of all people
   B. life-giver
   C. lover of fruit
   D. woman

---

**4.** In which order were Adam, Eve, and the serpent cursed?

   **A.** Adam, Eve, Serpent

   **B.** Eve, Adam, Serpent

   **C.** Serpent, Eve, Adam

   **D.** Kappa Alpha Order

## MATCHING

| | | |
|---|---|---|
| **1.** Sarah | a. King Ahasuerus | |
| **2.** Zipporah | b. Samuel | |
| **3.** Gilbert | c. Moses | |
| **4.** Rachel | d. Jacob | |
| **5.** Potiphar's Wife | e. David | |
| **6.** Esther | f. Abraham | ANSWERS p. 72 |
| **7.** Rebekah | g. Sullivan | |
| **8.** Michal | h. Joseph | |
| **9.** Hagar | i. Isaac | |
| **10.** Hannah | j. Ishmael | |

Q. What do John the Baptist and Winnie the Pooh have in common?

A. They both have the same middle name.

## SHORT ANSWER

1. Of whom was it said, "This one shall give us rest from our work and from the toil of our hands arising from the ground which the Lord has cursed"?

_____

2. Who said the following to whom? "Please let there be no strife between you and me, nor between my herdsmen and your herdsmen, for we are brothers."

_____

3. List the ten miraculous deeds that the Lord performed through Moses and Aaron before Pharaoh.

_____

_____

_____

4. Name Job's three friends. _____,

_____, _____

5. Define the following names of God.

ANSWERS
p. 73

   **A.** Abba _____

   **B.** Shaddai _____

   **C.** 'Elohim _____

**D.** 'Adonai _____

**E.** Yahweh _____

## FILL IN THE FAMILY TREE

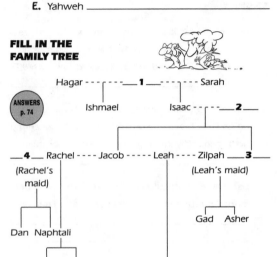

ANSWERS
p. 74

Hagar - - - - - **1** - - - - - - Sarah

Ishmael                 Isaac - - - - **2**

___ **4** ___ Rachel - - - - Jacob - - - - - Leah - - - - Zilpah ___ **3** ___

(Rachel's maid)                                    (Leah's maid)

Dan  Naphtali                          Gad  Asher

___ **5** ___ **6** ___

___ **7** ___ Simeon  Levi ___ **8** ___ Issachar  Zebulun

## TRUE OR FALSE

1. Miriam became leprous when she questioned God's speaking through Moses alone.

2. Sarah and Abraham had the same father.

ANSWERS
p. 75

3. Isaac loved Jacob and Rebekah loved Esau.

4. The phrase "Holiness to the Lord" appeared on a priest's turban.

5. Chedorlaomer was a Pokemon.

6. The sun obeyed Joshua's command to stand still.

7. Samson's wife was a Moabite.

8. Saul was made King by his people in Jerusalem.

9. Cyrus, the Persian King, declared that the captive Israelites should leave his land and build a temple for their Lord.

Famous (and not-so-famous) Figures ✦

**10.** The Philistines sold the people of Judah and Jerusalem to the Greeks.

## TALL TALE

One day a _____ man was walking down the
                    ADJECTIVE

street. He encountered a huge _____ and asked
                                    NOUN

it how it was feeling. It said it was very _____.
                                              EMOTION

So, the man wanted to help him. He took him to the nearby

_____ to get some ice cream, because
      STORE NAME

ice cream always makes you feel _____.
                                     EMOTION

The man picked _____, his favorite,
                  ICE CREAM FLAVOR

but the _____ just got a _____.
            NOUN                    BEVERAGE

This made the man _____ _____.
                      SUPERLATIVE      EMOTION

He had wanted to help the _____ but it wouldn't
                              NOUN

budge. So, he realized, some _____ just won't change
                                 NOUNS

no matter what you _____. Before continuing on his
                        VERB

way he _____ his ice cream and told the
          VERB (PAST TENSE)

_____ he hoped he would _____.
     NOUN                           COMMON PHRASE

Moral of the story: _____.
                         MORAL

1. **Jesus' birth to a virgin was predicted by which Old Testament prophet?**
   A. Daniel
   B. Isaiah
   C. Jeremiah
   D. Nebuchadnezzar

2. **Jesus' birth in Bethlehem was predicted by which Old Testament prophet?**
   A. Micah
   B. Isaiah
   C. 1-800-PSYCHIC hotline
   D. Ezekiel

ANSWERS
p. 76

3. **What did Tamar, Rahab, Ruth, and Mary have in common?**
   A. They all auditioned for The Spice Girls—a volunteer organization of women who placed spices in the tombs of those who had died.
   B. They are all in the genealogy of Jesus.
   C. They all sang songs to God's glory.
   D. They were all Jewish.

4. **What did Herod the tetrarch give to his wife's daughter for her birthday?**
   A. silk from the Orient
   B. a mustang convertible
   C. the head of John the Baptist
   D. the city of Tiberias

5. **Which Jewish sect did not believe in the resurrection of the dead?**
   A. the Pharisees
   B. the Sadducees
   C. the Zealots
   D. the Wannabes

## HOW ABOUT THAT!

Legend says that Luke, accepted writer of the gospel Luke and Acts, was an artist, and that in A.D. 590 Pope Gregory the Great used one of his paintings to lead a procession that stopped a plague!

### FILL IN THE BLANKS

1. Who was the first martyr? _____

2. This queen's servant was converted by Philip on the road from Jerusalem to Gaza: _____

3. On Paul's first missionary journey he traveled to _____ and _____.

4. The book of Philemon is written about a _____ _____.

## WORD BANK

> John    runaway slave    Galatia and Cyprus
>
> Candace, Queen of Ethiopia
>
> Sodom & Gomorrah

## MATCHING

1. Ethiopian Eunuch
2. Jesus (after the resurrection)
3. Saul
4. Jesus and Simon a Cyrenian
5. Willie Nelson

a. the Road to Damascus
b. the Road to Golgotha
c. the Road Again
d. the Road from Jerusalem to Gaza
e. the Road to Emmaus

## TRUE OR FALSE

1. Titus went to work with the Corinthians.

2. Paul tells the Galatians how he confronted Andrew face to face in Antioch.

3. Paul speaks of the Whole Armor of God in Ephesians.

4. Ricky Martin is living la vida loca.

5. Paul was married.

ANSWERS p. 77

---

# Top Ten Reasons God Created Eve

10. God worried that Adam would always be lost in the garden, because he hated to ask for directions.
9. God knew that Adam would one day need someone to straighten out his fig tie.
8. God knew that Adam would never buy a new fig leaf when his seat wore out and would therefore need Eve to get one for him.
7. God knew that Adam would never make a doctor's appointment for himself.
6. God knew that Adam would never remember which night was garbage night.
5. God knew that if the world was to be populated, men would never be able to handle childbearing.
4. As "Keeper of the Garden," Adam would never remember where he put his tools.
3. He had some extra parts left over.
2. As the Bible says, "It is not good for man to be alone!"
1. When God finished the creation of Adam, He stepped back, scratched His head and said, "I can do better than that."

6. Onesimus was a runaway slave of the household of Philemon.

7. Hebrews was written by Paul.

8. Joseph worried about how Mary's pregnancy would look to other people.

9. John wrote, in Revelation, that the church of Ephesus lost their love for Jesus.

10. Jezebel ordered that Elisha be killed.

Simon Peter's Nightmare

# ANSWERS TO:
## FAMOUS (AND NOT-SO-FAMOUS) FIGURES

## MULTIPLE CHOICE

| # ANSWER | REFERENCE |
|----------|-----------|
| 1. c | Genesis 1:2 |
| 2. b | |
| 3. b | |
| 4. c | Genesis 3:14–19 |

## MATCHING

| # ANSWER | REFERENCE |
|----------|-----------|
| 1. f | husband and wife—Genesis 17—18) |
| 2. c | husband and wife—Exodus 2:21 |
| 3. g | musical duo of the late nineteenth century |
| 4. d | husband and wife—Genesis 29:28 |
| 5. h | attempted seductress and victim of libel—Genesis 39 |

| # | ANSWER | REFERENCE |
|---|--------|-----------|
| 6. a | husband and wife—Esther 2:17 | |
| 7. i | husband and wife—Genesis 24:15ff | |
| 8. e | husband and wife—1 Samuel 18:27 | |
| 9. j | mother and son—Genesis 16 | |
| 10. b | mother and son—1 Samuel 1 | |

## SHORT ANSWER

| # | ANSWER | REFERENCE |
|---|--------|-----------|
| 1. | Noah | Genesis 5:29 |
| 2. | Jacob and Esau | |
| 3. | Water in the Nile turned to blood | Exodus 7–11 |
| | Frogs invade the land | |
| | Lice | |
| | Flies | |
| | Plague of boils | |
| | Plague of hail | |
| | Plague of locusts | |
| | Darkness over Egypt | |
| | Death of First Born | |

## SHORT
## ANSWER—cont'd

| # ANSWER | REFERENCE |
|---|---|
| 4. Eliphaz | Job 2:11 |
| Bildad | |
| Zophar | |
| 5. Abba—Daddy | |
| Shaddai—Almighty; All-Powerful God | |
| 'Elohim—God; The Creator | |
| 'Adonai—Lord; The Master | |
| Yahweh—LORD; the most intimate name for God; | |
| the Israelites wrote it without the vowels: YHWH | |

## FILL IN THE
## FAMILY TREE

| # ANSWER |
|---|
| 1. Abraham |
| 2. Rebekah |
| 3. Esau |
| 4. Bilhah |
| 5. Joseph |
| 6. Benjamin |

## # ANSWER

7. Reuben, the firstborn
8. Judah—Genesis 36 and Matthew 1

## TRUE OR FALSE

| # ANSWER | REFERENCE |
|----------|-----------|
| 1. True | Numbers 12:2, 10 |
| 2. True | Genesis 20:12 |
| 3. False; Isaac loved Esau and Rebekah loved Jacob | Genesis 25:28 |
| 4. True | Exodus 28:36–37 |
| 5. False; King of Elam | Genesis 14:9 |
| 6. True | Joshua 10:12–13 |
| 7. False; Philistine | Judges 14:2 |
| 8. False; Gilgal | 1 Samuel 11:15 |
| 9. True | Ezra 1:1–4 |
| 10. True | Joel 3:6 |

Q. Why did Elijah pour water over the steer on the altar?

A. To make gravy!

## MULTIPLE CHOICE

| # ANSWER | REFERENCE |
| --- | --- |
| 1. b | Isaiah 7:14 |
| 2. a | Micah 5:2 |
| 3. b | Matthew 1:3,5,16 |
| 4. c | Matthew 14:3–11 |
| 5. b | Matthew 22:23 |

## FILL IN THE BLANKS

| # ANSWER | REFERENCE |
| --- | --- |
| 1. Stephen | Acts 7:59 |
| 2. Candace, Queen of Ethiopia | Acts 8:27 |
| 3. Galatia and Cyprus | Acts 13–14 |
| 4. runaway slave | Philemon 1 |

## MATCHING

| # ANSWER | REFERENCE |
| --- | --- |
| 1. d | Acts 8:26 |
| 2. e | Luke 24:13 |
| 3. a | Acts 9:3 |
| 4. b | Mark 15:21 |
| 5. c | |

# TRUE OR FALSE

| # ANSWER | REFERENCE |
|---|---|
| 1. True | 2 Corinthians 8:16–17 |
| 2. False; Peter | Galatians 2:11 |
| 3. True | Ephesians 6:10–19 |
| 4. True | |

5. Traditionally believed to be False. However, a close study of Philippians 4 raises doubts. In Phil 4:3 Paul addresses his ''true companion,'' which is, in the greek, the word used for spouse—it literally means ''yoke fellow.''

| 6. True | Philemon 1 |
|---|---|

7. The author of Hebrews is unknown.

| 8. True | Matthew 1 |
|---|---|
| 9. True | Revelation 2:1–7 |
| 10. False; Elijah | 1 Kings 19:2 |

---

Q. Who was the poorest man in the Bible?

A. Nickledemus!

---

# I Believe in Miracles

## SHORT ANSWER

1. What is the first miracle? _____

_____

2. How did Enoch die? _____

_____

3. Where did God enact the miracle of confusing language? _____

4. What did God do to Pharaoh's house when Sarah stayed there under the guise of Abraham's sister?

_____

_____

5. What miracle occurred when God changed Sarai's name to Sarah? _____

6. What did the angels do to the men who approached Lot's home? _____

7. How did God destroy Sodom? _____

_____

8. How did Lot's wife die? _____

**MULTIPLE CHOICE**

1. **What was Moses doing when God appeared to him in the burning bush?**
   A. drawing water from his father-in-law's well
   B. tending his father-in-law's sheep
   C. tending his own sheep
   D. commenting that his throat was on fire

---

# HOW ABOUT THAT!

John, in his gospel, reports on seven miracles of Jesus. He also lists seven "I am" statements from Jesus. Both of these are used to prove that Jesus was God.

---

2. **Why was Moses' rod turned into a serpent?**
   A. to impress Pharaoh
   B. for extra protection from Pharaoh
   C. so that the Egyptians would believe God had appeared to Moses
   D. to shock the people into obedience

3. **What happened when Moses put his hand in his bosom?**

**A.** it turned leprous
**B.** it fell off
**C.** he passed out
**D.** it bled but no skin was broken

4. **Which miracles did Moses and God talk about at the burning bush?**
   **A.** his rod turning into a serpent
   **B.** parting the Red Sea
   **C.** his hand becoming leprous
   **D.** water from the Nile turning to blood

ANSWERS
p. 95

5. **When Moses and Aaron turned the water to blood how much water was affected?**
   **A.** just the water in the Nile
   **B.** the water in the Nile, as well as ponds and tributaries
   **C.** the water in the Nile, ponds, tributaries, buckets and pitchers
   **D.** only the water at Pharaoh's feet

6. **Pharaoh's magicians imitated which of the Lord's miraculous plagues on Egypt?**
   **A.** frogs
   **B.** lice
   **C.** darkness
   **D.** bubonic

7. **What did Aaron strike that became lice?**
   **A.** a nerve
   **B.** stone
   **C.** wood
   **D.** dust

8. **Pharaoh's magicians gave credit to whom for the plague of lice?**
   A. Baal
   B. God
   C. Ra
   D. James Preston at 243 3rd Ave.

9. **Which of the following miracles occurred on the way to Sinai?**
   A. healing the bitter waters
   B. the miracle on 34th street
   C. quail provided by God
   D. victory over Amalek

10. **Which of the following were miracles of Elijah?**
    A. multiplies oil
    B. multiplies food
    C. restores rains
    D. purifies poison

11. **Which of the following were miracles of Elisha?**
    A. heals Naaman
    B. supplies and increases oil
    C. brings a drought
    D. destroys alter of Baal

12. **Which of the following miracles happened in Daniel?**
    A. Writing on the wall
    B. idol of Dagon falls on its face
    C. King Nebuchadnezzar's madness
    D. Israel delivered from captivity

## Top Ten Plagues Not Inflicted on the Egyptians

**10.** Bad rap music

**9.** Ingrown toenails

**8.** Excessive navel lint

**7.** Bad hair days

**6.** Sluggish Internet providers

**5.** High insurance premiums

**4.** Overpopulation of Elvis impersonators

**3.** Allergies and leg cramps

**2.** Traffic delays due to construction

**1.** Grocery carts with one "bad" wheel

## FILL IN THE BLANKS

1. God miraculously led his people by a _____ _____ _____ by day and a _____ _____ _____ by night.

2. The Lord said to Moses: "Lift up your _____, and stretch out your _____ over the _____ and divide it. And the children of Israel shall go on _____ _____ through the midst of the _____.

3. Moses cast a _____ into the waters at Marah to make them _____.

4. The Israelites complained that they would rather be in Egypt where they had _____.

5. The Israelites were to gather manna only _____ _____ _____ _____, except on the _____ day, when they were to gather _____.

6. In addition to manna, God also provided _____ for the Israelites to eat in the desert.

ANSWERS p. 96

7. _____ came out of the _____ when Moses struck it with his _____.

8. The Israelites defeated _____ as long as Moses _____ _____ _____ _____ _____ _____.

---

Q. Why was Peter unable to maintain his walk on the water?
A. He had a sinking feeling it wasn't going to last.

---

## WORD BANK

tree     quail     water     Amalek

rod     wet ground     sweet

food     sixth     rock

held his hands in the air     enough for one day

star     rainbow     dry ground

hand     sea     milk     eighth

pillar of fire     pillar of cloud

double     Abraham

## UNSCRAMBLE (the objects of miracles)

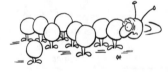

1. Erd Ase

2. Nideogs Elefec

3. Ticy fo Reijoch

4. Loi

5. Dojarn Evirr

6. Nilos Ned

7. Niew

8. Mostr

ANSWERS
p. 97

1. What happened to Aaron's rod that signified his family should be the priestly family? _____

_____

2. What did God send among the Israelites when they complained about their food and water? _____

_____

3. What did Balaam's donkey say to him when he saw the angel? _____

_____

4. How did Balaam react when the donkey spoke to him? _____

5. How did God separate the waters of the Jordan river? _____

_____

6. What did the Israelites do differently on their seventh trip around Jericho? _____

_____

_____

**7.** Who commanded the sun to stand still, and it did?

_____

_____

**8.** God chased and killed the Amorites with what force of nature? _____

_____

**MULTIPLE
CHOICE**

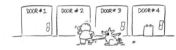

1. **Jesus turned water into wine at:**
   **A.** a wedding in Nazareth, his hometown
   **B.** a wedding in Cana of Galilee
   **C.** Jehosaphat's Bar and Grill
   **D.** a wedding in Damascus

2. **Jesus healed the nobleman's son in:**
   **A.** Cana of Galilee
   **B.** Timbuktu
   **C.** Damascus
   **D.** Bethsaida

ANSWERS
p. 98

3. **Jesus cast out an unclean spirit while preaching in a synagogue after it said to him:**
   **A.** I am a legion, and I will destroy your work in the world.
   **B.** I am a legion, and I know who you are—Son of Man.

**C.** I been noticin' you.
**D.** I know who You are—the Holy One of God!

4. **Jesus healed Peter's mother of:**
   **A.** a demon
   **B.** a tumor
   **C.** a high fever
   **D.** the stress Peter caused her

5. **Whose boat was Jesus in when he miraculously caught a great number of fish?**
   **A.** Simon Peter's
   **B.** John's
   **C.** the Love Boat
   **D.** Andrew's

6. **The man who was let in through the roof to see Jesus was:**
    A. dead
    B. paralyzed
    C. sick with a high fever
    D. a bad roofer

7. **When Jesus healed the man at the pool of Bethesda, he told:**
    A. the Pharisees, who sought to know where he lived
    B. the paparazzi, who sought to take a picture of him
    C. the Roman government, who sought to silence him
    D. the Jews, who sought to kill him

8. **The centurion believed that Jesus only had to do what for his servant to be healed?**
    A. say the word
    B. touch him
    C. the hokey-pokey
    D. send one of his disciples

ANSWERS
p. 98

**TRUE OR FALSE**

1. Jesus raised the son of the widow of Nain from the dead.

2. Jesus calmed the storm the same day that he told the parable of the sower.

**3.** The hemorrhaging woman was healed after she told Jesus she believed that he was the Christ.

**4.** The man whose daughter was healed was the ruler of the centurions.

**5.** Jesus healed two blind men who followed him and said, "Son of David, have mercy on us!"

**6.** Jesus fed the five thousand barley loaves and fish.

**7.** Jesus and the twelve disciples starred in the musical about their lives called *Godspell*.

**8.** After Jesus walked on the water, he got in the boat with the disciples and immediately the boat was at the place where they were going.

**9.** Jesus told the mother of the demon-possessed girl that it is not good to throw the children's food to the dogs.

**10.** To heal the deaf and dumb man, Jesus put His fingers in his ears, spat, touched his tongue, sighed and said, "Be opened," and he was healed.

---

Q. What time of day was Adam born?
A. Before Eve.

---

## MATCHING

1. deaf and dumb man healed
2. man born blind healed
3. woman bound by Satan healed
4. man with dropsy healed
5. Lazarus raised from the dead
6. ten lepers healed
7. second catch of fish
8. graves opened at Calvary
9. Jesus' graveclothes were undisturbed
10. two disciples see the resurrected Jesus

a. Matthew
b. Mark
c. Luke
d. John

ANSWERS p. 99

# ANSWERS TO:
# I BELIEVE IN MIRACLES

## SHORT ANSWER

| # ANSWER | REFERENCE |
| --- | --- |
| 1. Creation | Genesis 1 |
| 2. He didn't. | Genesis 5:19–24 |
| 3. Tower of Babel | Genesis 11:1–9 |
| 4. plagued them | Genesis 12:14–20 |
| 5. fertility | Genesis 17:15–16 |
| 6. struck them with blindness | Genesis 19:9–11 |
| 7. with brimstone and fire | Genesis 19:24 |
| 8. She turned into salt. | Genesis 19:26 |

## MULTIPLE CHOICE

| # ANSWER | REFERENCE |
| --- | --- |
| 1. b | Exodus 3:1 |
| 2. c | Exodus 4:5 |
| 3. a | Exodus 4:6 |
| 4. a,c,d | Exodus 4 |
| 5. c | Exodus 7:19 |

## MULTIPLE CHOICE—cont'd

| # ANSWER | REFERENCE |
|----------|-----------|
| 6. a | Exodus 8:7–11 |
| 7. d | Exodus 8:17 |
| 8. b | Exodus 8:19 |
| 9. a,c,d | Exodus 15, 16 |
| 10. b,c | 1 Kings 17, 18 |
| 11. a,b | 2 Kings 4:1–10; |
| | 2 Kings 5:1–11 |
| 12. a,c | Daniel 4, 5 |

## FILL IN THE BLANKS

| # ANSWER | REFERENCE |
|----------|-----------|
| 1. pillar of cloud, pillar of fire | Exodus 13:21–22 |
| 2. rod, hand, sea, dry ground, sea | Exodus 14:16 |
| 3. tree, sweet | Exodus 15:26 |
| 4. food | Exodus 16:3 |
| 5. enough for one day, sixth, double | Exodus 16:4–5 |
| 6. quail | Exodus 16:7–13 |
| 7. Water, rock, rod | Exodus 17:6 |
| 8. Amalek, held his hands in the air | Exodus 17:8–13 |

## UNSCRAMBLE

| # ANSWER | REFERENCE |
|----------|-----------|
| 1. Red Sea | Exodus 14 |
| 2. Gideon's Fleece | Judges 6 |
| 3. City of Jericho | Joshua 6–8 |
| 4. Oil | 2 Kings 4 |
| 5. Jordan River | Joshua 3, 4 |
| 6. Lions' Den | Daniel 6 |
| 7. Wine | John 2 |
| 8. Storm | Mark 4 |

## SHORT ANSWER

| # ANSWER | REFERENCE |
|----------|-----------|
| 1. this rod put forth buds and blossoms | Numbers 17 |
| 2. fiery serpents | Numbers 21:4–9 |
| 3. What have I done to you, that you have struck me these three times? | Numbers 22:28 |

| # ANSWER | REFERENCE |
|---|---|
| 4. answered his question | Numbers 22:29 |
| 5. the elders put their feet in and the water piled in a heap | Joshua 3–4 |
| 6. shouted | Joshua 6 |
| 7. Joshua | Joshua 10:12–13 |
| 8. hailstorm | Joshua 10:10–11 |

## MULTIPLE CHOICE

| # ANSWER | REFERENCE |
|---|---|
| 1. b | John 2 |
| 2. a | John 4:46 |
| 3. d | Luke 4:34 |
| 4. c | Luke 4:38 |
| 5. a | Luke 5 |
| 6. b | Luke 5 |
| 7. d | John 5 |
| 8. a | Luke 7 |

## TRUE OR FALSE

| # ANSWER | REFERENCE |
|---|---|
| 1. True | Luke 7 |
| 2. True | Mark 4 |
| 3. False; touched the hem of Jesus' garment | Matthew 9 |
| 4. False; ruler of the synagogue | Luke 8:40–56 |
| 5. True | Matthew 9 |
| 6. True | John 6 |
| 7. False | |
| 8. True | John 6:21 |
| 9. True | Matthew 15:26 |
| 10. True | Mark 7 |

## MATCHING

| # ANSWER | REFERENCE |
|---|---|
| 1. b | Mark 7:31–37 |
| 2. d | John 9 |
| 3. c | Luke 13:10–17 |
| 4. c | Luke 14:1–6 |
| 5. d | John 11 |
| 6. c | Luke 17:11–19 |

| # ANSWER | REFERENCE |
|----------|-----------|
| 7. d | John 21:1–14 |
| 8. a | Matthew 27:52–53 |
| 9. d | John 20:2–10 |
| 10. c | Luke 24:13–35 |

# THE MIRACLES OF JESUS CHRIST

1. Cleansing a Leper — Matthew 8:2; Mark 1:40; Luke 5:12

2. Healing a Centurion's Servant (of paralysis) — Matthew 8:5; Luke 7:1

3. Healing Peter's Mother-in-Law — Matthew 8:14; Mark 1:30; Luke 4:38

4. Healing the Sick at Evening — Matthew 8:16; Mark 1:32; Luke 4:40

5. Stilling the Storm — Mathew 8:23; Mark 4:35; Luke 8:22

6. Demons Entering a Herd of Swine — Mathew 8:28; Mark 5:1; Luke 8:26

7. Healing a Paralytic — Mathew 9:2; Mark 2:3; Luke 5:18

8. Raising the Ruler's Daughter — Mathew 9:18, 23; Mark 5:22, 35; Luke 8:40,49

9. Healing the Hemorrhaging Woman — Mathew 9:20; Mark 5:25; Luke 8:43

10. Healing Two Blind Men — Mathew 9:27

11. Curing a Demon-possessed, Mute Man — Mathew 9:32

12. Healing a Man's Withered Hand — Mathew 12:9; Mark 3:1; Luke 6:6

13. Curing a Demon-possessed, Blind and Mute Man — Mathew 12:22; Luke 11:14

14. Feeding the Five Thousand — Matthew 14:13; Mark 6:30; Luke 9:10; John 6:1

| 15. | Walking on the Sea | Matthew 14:25; Mark 6:48; John 6:19 |
| 16. | Healing the Gentile Woman's Daughter | Matthew 15:21; Mark 7:24 |
| 17. | Feeding the Four Thousand | Matthew 15:32; Mark 8:1 |
| 18. | Healing the Epileptic Boy | Matthew 17:14; Mark 9:17; Luke 9:38 |
| 19. | Temple Tax in the Fish's Mouth | Matthew 17:24 |
| 20. | Healing Two Blind Men | Matthew 20:30; Mark 10:46; Luke 18:35 |
| 21. | Withering the Fig Tree | Matthew 21:18; Mark 11:12 |
| 22. | Casting Out an Unclean Spirit | Mark 1:23; Luke 14:33 |
| 23. | Healing a Deaf Mute | Mark 7:31 |
| 24. | Healing a Blind Paralytic at Bethsaida | Mark 8:22 |
| 25. | Escape from the Hostile Multitude | Luke 4:30 |
| 26. | Draught of Fish | Luke 5:1 |
| 27. | Raising of a Widow's Son at Nain | Luke 7:11 |
| 28. | Healing the Infirm, Bent Woman | Luke 13:11 |
| 29. | Healing a Man with Dropsy | Luke 14:1 |
| 30. | Cleansing the Ten Lepers | Luke 17:11 |
| 31. | Restoring a Servant's Ear | Luke 22:51 |
| 32. | Turning Water into Wine | John 2:1 |
| 33. | Healing the Nobleman's Son (of fever) | John 4:46 |

# Say a Little Prayer for Me

**SHORT ANSWER**

1. Paul prayed for what after being threatened by Jewish leaders in Acts? _____

2. How did the Lord first describe Saul of Tarsus to Ananias? _____

3. Paul commanded Simon the Sorcerer to pray for forgiveness from what? _____

4. Paul prayed and healed whom on the island of Malta? _____

5. The apostles named two men—Barsabbas and Matthias—and then prayed about what? _____

_____

6. Paul prayed over Tabitha for what? _____

_____

7. The apostles chose seven men to care for widows, and then prayed over them with what result?

_____

8. What were Paul and Silas doing when their chains fell off in prison? _____

_____

## MATCHING

1. Abraham

2. David

3. Beniah

4. Gideon

5. Asa

ANSWERS
p. 120

6. Hezekiah

7. Dion Warwick

8. Amos

a. "Lord, it is nothing for you to help . . . do not let this man prevail against You!"

b. "May [the Lord] be with Solomon, and make his throne greater than the throne of my lord King David."

c. "If you will . . . give your maidservant a male child . . . no razor shall come upon his head."

d. "The moment I wake up, before I put on my makeup, I say a little prayer for you."

e. "Lord God of Abraham, Isaac, and Israel, let it be known this day that You are God in Israel and I am your servant."

f. "Oh, that Ishmael might live before You!"

g. "If You will save Israel by my hand as You have said— look . . ."

h. "O Lord, I pray, turn the counsel of Ahithophel into foolishness."

9. Hannah

i. "Remember now, O Lord, I pray, how I have walked before You in truth and with a loyal heart, and have done what was good in your sight."

10. Elijah

j. "O Lord God, cease, I pray! Oh, that Jacob may stand, for he is small!"

---

# HOW ABOUT THAT!

Many Roman Catholics pray on November 2 or All Souls' Day to hasten the transition of their dead loved ones from Purgatory to Heaven.

---

**MULTIPLE CHOICE**

1. **When Elisha prayed for the Lord to open the servant's eyes, his servant saw:**
   **A.** hills full of horses and chariots of fire
   **B.** towers crumbling
   **C.** steam rising off the oceans
   **D.** Elisha

---

2. When he prayed before the Lord, Hezekiah spread out:
   A. a fleece
   B. some "I Can't Believe It's Not Butter" on a roll
   C. a map
   D. a letter from King Sennacherib

3. Whose request, "O that you would bless me and enlarge my territory," did God grant?
   A. David's
   B. Jabez's
   C. Benji's
   D. Ahab's

ANSWERS
p. 121

4. When Jacob prayed because of his fear of Esau, he did what to his people for protection?
   A. divided them into two groups, so one could run away
   B. gave them skins and told them to hide among the flocks
   C. gave them invisible suits, so that Esau wouldn't see them
   D. camped in the valley, so that they would see an army coming over the hills

5. What was Jacob's attitude when he prayed for his sons?
   A. proud
   B. sassy
   C. bereaved
   D. lonely

# Top Ten
# Prayer Endings

**10.** Thank you and goodnight!

**9.** See ya!

**8.** Peace Out!

**7.** Hasta la vista, baby!

**6.** You have been a great audience, thank you!

**5.** I'm outta here!

**4.** Later, dude!

**3.** Until we meet again!

**2.** Watch your head on the way out!

**1.** Adios, amigo!

6. **Where did Jehoshaphat pray for Judah?**
   A. in Jerusalem, in the King's court
   B. in front of the new courtyard at the new Temple
   C. in the privacy of his tent
   D. he didn't

7. **How did the people of Bethel ask the Lord about fasting?**
   A. they offered sacrifices themselves
   B. they asked their leaders
   C. via e-mail
   D. they sent two leaders (and their men) to ask the priests and prophets

8. **What did Joshua pray after Israel defeated the Amorites?**
   A. that the Amonites wouldn't be too mad
   B. thanksgiving to God for his protection
   C. for the sun to stand still
   D. that the Amorites would be punished for their sins

**TRUE OR FALSE**

1. The Hebrew word "Amen" means "I now conclude."

2. The Egyptian plan for prayer was to coerce the gods.

3. Lot prayed that his wife would become like "the salt of the earth."

4. When the Israelites worshipped the Golden Calf, Moses prayed, "Oh God, free me from service to these pagan people!"

5. Moses called on God to not respect the offering of a priest in a competition at the altar.

6. Naomi prayed that her daughters-in-law would remarry.

7. Elijah asked to be known as God's servant when he challenged the prophets of Baal.

8. After the pagan sailors threw Jonah overboard, they gloated in victory and cursed God.

**9.** Jesus prayed in the Garden of Gethsemane that God's will be done.

**10.** Isaiah, after being cleansed with coal, said to God, "Here am I, send me."

## FILL IN THE BLANKS

**1.** After Elijah's victory over the pagan prophets of _____, he prayed, "It is enough! Now, Lord, take my _____, for I am no better than my _____."

**2.** Jonah _____ while in the belly of the fish, and then preached to _____, whom he feared would _____.

**3.** When _____ confronted King David of his sin with _____, he confessed, "I have sinned against the _____."

**4.** Ezra confessed his sin _____, which led to a _____.

**5.** After Abraham's victory over the raiders who had captured his _____ Lot, _____ prayed a blessing over him.

**6.** Naomi's neighbors praised God for giving her a

_____.

**7.** The Queen of Sheba praised _____ for

making _____ king.

**8.** Solomon praised God for his nation's _____.

**9.** Ezra praised God that a _____ ruler provided

_____ to restore the _____.

**10.** Daniel asked God to _____ _____'s

_____.

## WORD BANK

| | | | |
|---|---|---|---|
| grandson | Baal | Lord | pagan |
| life | nephew | God | Temple |
| reveal | dream | Melchizedek | |
| Solomon | peace | fathers | |
| Nathan | publicly | prayed | |
| Bathsheba | repent | revival | |
| funds | Nebuchadnezzar's | Ninevah | |

### FILL IN THE BLANKS

1. David prays, in Psalm 16, "In your _____ is fullness of joy."

2. After the dedication of the house of David, he says (in Psalm 30), "I will give thanks to you _____."

3. The author of Psalm 38 tells God he will be in _____ over his sins.

4. During his exile in Judah, David wrote Psalm 63 saying, "My soul shall be _____."

---

**5.** In Psalm 3, David describes the protection of God as

a _____.

**6.** Psalm 71 begs God to, "Be my strong _____."

**CLUE:** God desires our _____.

ANSWERS p. 123

## WORD BANK

| | |
|---|---|
| forever | refuge |
| anguish | shield |
| satisfied | presence |

## MATCHING

1. 'atar
2. palal
3. paga'
4. shama'
5. sha'al
6. sha<sup>e</sup>la
7. sa'al
8. hanan
9. 'ana
10. na'

a. to hear or listen to
b. I pray.
c. to beg
d. to desire
e. to answer
f. to intercede
g. to pray
h. to beseech
i. to request
j. to entreat

ANSWERS p. 123

1. **The rosary is a Roman Catholic prayer consisting of fifteen sets of ten:**
   A. bicep curls
   B. Hail Marys
   C. rosarys
   D. Mother Marys

2. **What book contains morning and evening prayers, as well as thirty-nine articles of religion:**
   A. The English Book of Prayer
   B. The Westminster Confession of Faith
   C. The Complete Guide to WWJD?
   D. Book of Common Prayer

3. **In Roman Catholic theology, prayers for the dead are for those people who are in:**
   A. Purgatory
   B. Hell
   C. Heaven
   D. Limbo

4. **Tibetan Buddhists use what when reciting mantras:**
   A. prayer chains
   B. prayer wheel
   C. hula hoops
   D. prayer books

---

5. **Which of the following statements is found in the Lord's prayer:**
   **A.** not my will but Thine be done
   **B.** give us this day our daily bread
   **C.** do unto us as we have done unto others
   **D.** I'm in the Lord's army

6. **What famous site in Jerusalem is the location of many Jewish prayers:**
   **A.** the temple of Jerusalem
   **B.** the market place
   **C.** the Wailing Wall
   **D.** the Church of the Sacred

ANSWERS
p. 124

**TRUE OR FALSE**

1. Paul says that women should never pray aloud at church.

2. All early believers prayed in tongues.

3. Paul says we should pray "always."

4. Christians should pray for their rulers so that life will be quiet and peaceable in godliness and reverence.

5. The Holy Spirit is not involved with human prayers.

# ANSWERS TO:
## SAY A LITTLE PRAYER FOR ME

## SHORT ANSWER

| # ANSWER | REFERENCE |
|----------|-----------|
| 1. boldness | Acts 4:23–31 |
| 2. he is praying | Acts 9:11 |
| 3. the thought in his heart | Acts 8:22 |
| 4. Publius' father | Acts 28:8 |
| 5. which one of the two should replace Judas | Acts 1:24 |
| 6. that she would be raised from the dead | Acts 9:40 |
| 7. the Word of God spread | Acts 6:7 |
| 8. praying and singing hymns | Acts 16:25 |

## MATCHING

| # ANSWER | REFERENCE |
|----------|-----------|
| 1. f | Genesis 17:18 |
| 2. h | 2 Samuel 15:31 |
| 3. b | 1 Kings 1:47 |
| 4. g | Judges 6:36 |
| 5. a | 2 Chronicles 14:11 |
| 6. i | 2 Kings 20:3 |

| # ANSWER | REFERENCE |
|----------|-----------|
| 7. d | |
| 8. j | Amos 7:2 |
| 9. c | 1 Samuel 1:11 |
| 10. e | 1 Kings 18:36 |

## MULTIPLE CHOICE

| # ANSWER | REFERENCE |
|----------|-----------|
| 1. a | 2 Kings 6:17 |
| 2. d | 2 Kings 19:14 |
| 3. b | 1 Chronicles 4:10 |
| 4. a | Genesis 32:7-12 |
| 5. c | Genesis 43:14 |
| 6. b | 2 Chronicles 20:5 |
| 7. d | Zechariah 7:3 |
| 8. c | Joshua 10:12 |

## TRUE OR FALSE

| # ANSWER | REFERENCE |
|----------|-----------|
| 1. False | "Let it be" |
| 2. True | |
| 3. False; she became a pillar of salt | Genesis 19:26 |
| 4. False; he confessed their sin | Exodus 32:31 |

## TRUE OR FALSE—cont'd

| # | ANSWER | REFERENCE |
|---|--------|-----------|
| 5. | True | Numbers 16:15 |
| 6. | True | Ruth 1:9 |
| 7. | True | 1 Kings 18:36 |
| 8. | False; They prayed. | Jonah 1:14 |
| 9. | True | |
| 10. | True | Isaiah 6:8 |

## FILL IN THE BLANKS

| # | ANSWER | REFERENCE |
|---|--------|-----------|
| 1. | Baal, life, fathers | 1 Kings 19:4 |
| 2. | prayed, Ninevah, repent | Jonah 2–3 |
| 3. | Nathan, Bathsheba, Lord | 2 Samuel 12:13 |
| 4. | publicly, revival | Ezra 9–10 |
| 5. | nephew, Melchizedek | Genesis 14:20 |
| 6. | grandson | Ruth 4:14 |
| 7. | God, Solomon | 1 Kings 10:9 |
| 8. | peace | 1 Kings 8:56 |
| 9. | pagan, funds, Temple | Ezra 7:27 |
| 10. | reveal Nebuchadnezzar's dream | Daniel 2:20 |

## FILL IN THE BLANKS

| # | ANSWER |
|---|--------|
| 1. | presence |
| 2. | forever |
| 3. | anguish |
| 4. | satisfied |
| 5. | shield |
| 6. | refuge |

God desires our: **Praise**

## MATCHING

| # | ANSWER |
|---|--------|
| 1. | j |
| 2. | g |
| 3. | f |
| 4. | a |
| 5. | c |
| 6. | i |
| 7. | d |
| 8. | h |
| 9. | e |
| 10. | b |

| # | ANSWER |
|---|--------|
| 1. | b |
| 2. | d |
| 3. | a |
| 4. | b |
| 5. | b |
| 6. | c |

**TRUE OR FALSE**

| # | ANSWER | REFERENCE |
|---|--------|-----------|
| 1. | False; women can pray aloud | 1 Corinthians 11 |
| 2. | False; some | 1 Corinthians 14 |
| 3. | True | Ephesians 6:18 |
| 4. | True | 1 Timothy 2 |
| 5. | False; makes intercession for us | Romans 8:26 |

As long as there are tests, there will always be prayer in school!

# PRAYERS OF THE BIBLE

Abijah's army (for victory) ........ 2 Chronicles 13:14
Abraham (for a son) ................. Genesis 15:1–6
Abraham (for Ishmael) ............. Genesis 17:18–21
Abraham (for Sodom) ........... Genesis 18:20–32
Abraham (for Abimelech) .......... Genesis 20:17
Abraham's servant
   (for guidance) ............. Genesis 24:12–52
Asa (for victory) ....................... 2 Chronicles 14:11

Cain (for mercy) ...................... Genesis 4:13–15
Centurion (for his servant) ........ Matthew 8:5–13
Christians (for Peter) ................. Acts 12:5–12
Christians (for kings in authority)... 1 Timothy 2:1, 2
Corinthians (for Paul)................ 2 Corinthians 1:9–11
Cornelius (for enlightenment) ...... Acts 10:1–33
Criminal (for salvation) ............. Luke 23:42, 43

Daniel (for the Jews)................. Daniel 9:3–19
Daniel (for knowledge) ............. Daniel 2:17–23
David (for blessing) ............... 2 Samuel 7:18–29
David (for help) ....................... 1 Samuel 23:10–13
David (for guidance) ................. 2 Samuel 2:1
David (for grace) ..................... Psalm 25:16
David (for justice) .................... Psalm 9:17–20
Disciples (for boldness) ............. Acts 4:24–31

Elijah (for drought and rain)........ James 5:17, 18
Elijah (for the raising to
   life of the widow's son) ........ 1 Kings 17:20–23
Elijah (for triumph over Baal) ...... 1 Kings 18:36–38
Elijah (for death) .................... 1 Kings 19:4

Samuel (for Israel) ..................... 1 Samuel 7:5–12
Solomon (for wisdom) .............. 1 Kings 3:6–14

Tax collector (for mercy)  ............ Luke 18:13

Zechariah (for a son) .................. Luke 1:13

# Tell Me
# a Story

## FILL IN THE BLANKS

1. The first parable told in the Gospel of Matthew is the parable of the _____.

2. In the Parable of the Sower, seed fell: _____ _____ _____, _____ _____ _____, _____, and _____ _____ _____.

3. When Jesus explained the purpose of parables, he said, "Therefore I speak to them in parables because _____ they do not _____, and _____ they do not _____, nor do they understand."

4. The _____ asked Jesus to explain why he spoke in parables, and he told them they were _____.

5. In the Parable of the Wheat and Tares, Jesus said, "The kingdom of _____ is like a _____ who sowed _____ seed in his field; but while the man _____, his enemy came and sowed _____ among the wheat and went his way."

**6.** In the Parable of the Wheat and Tares the man _____ the tares and put the wheat in his _____.

**7.** The kingdom of heaven is like a _____ seed, which becomes a tree in which the birds of the air _____ in its branches.

**8.** The kingdom of heaven is like _____ which a woman took and hid in her _____ until it was all _____.

### WORD BANK

| | | | |
|---|---|---|---|
| barn | seeing | mustard | citizens |
| unmerciful servant | | sunflower | meal |
| basket | heaven | hear | man |
| good | leavened | disciples | slept |
| tares | see | sower | by the wayside |
| leaven | in stony places | | in the lake |
| burned | hearing | smell | rotten |
| nest | on good ground | | blessed |
| | rocked | tails | |

## TRUE OR FALSE

1. Jesus did not explain the Parable of the Sower.

2. When Jesus spoke in parables, he spoke things that were kept secret from the foundation of the world.

3. Jesus explained the Parable of the Wheat and Tares to all the people who heard the parable.

4. In the Parable of the Hidden Treasure, the man sold all he had to buy a field.

5. In the Parable of the Pearl of Great Price, the man sold all he had to buy a pearl.

6. In the Parable of the Ugly Duckling, a huge man sings "fee fie fo fum" while two children eat a house made of candy.

7. In the Parable of the Dragnet, God Himself will separate the wicked from the just.

8. In telling the Parable of the Dragnet, Jesus asked the disciples if they understood "all these things."

9. According to the Gospel of Matthew, when Jesus finished telling the Parables of the Sower, Wheat and Tares, Mustard Seed, and Dragnet, he left for his home, Nazareth.

10. The point of the Parable of the Lost Sheep is the God cares about every one of his children.

1. **In the Parable of the Lost Sheep, Jesus says that one should not despise children because:**
   A. their angels always see the face of God
   B. they possess the spirit that we should aim for
   C. they're just so cute
   D. their actions reflect the teachings of their parents

2. **How many sheep did the shepherd have?**
   A. 1000
   B. 100
   C. 50
   D. none, he lost them all

ANSWERS
p. 148

3. **The Parable of the Unforgiving Servant was told in response to the question:**
   A. "How do you catch a Pokémon?"
   B. "Who will be the greatest in the kingdom of Heaven?"
   C. "Who will sit at the right hand of Jesus in Heaven?"
   D. "How often shall my brother sin against me, and I forgive him?"

4. **The Parable of the Unforgiving Servant ends with the servant:**

**A.** forgiven

**B.** standing next to a plane, saying, "This is the beginning of a beautiful friendship."

**C.** in jail and tortured

**D.** dead

5. **It is harder for a rich man to enter heaven than:**

**A.** to find a needle in a haystack

**B.** a camel to go through the eye of a needle

**C.** a needle to go through the eye of a camel

**D.** a sheep to find its way back to the fold

# HOW ABOUT THAT!

The book of John contains no parables!

6. **In the Parable of the Workers in the Vineyard, the agreed wage was:**

**A.** a denarius a day

**B.** ten denarii a day

**C.** ten denarii a week

**D.** four pigs and one chicken per day

7. **Jesus ends the Parable of the Workers in the Vineyard by saying:**

**A.** All that are called are chosen.
**B.** I'm the king of the world.
**C.** Many are called but few are chosen.
**D.** The owner may choose those that it pleases him to choose.

**8. The workers complained about**
   **A.** the heat
   **B.** the people the owner chose
   **C.** vacation days not rolling over
   **D.** the amount of pay

ANSWERS
p. 148

## SHORT ANSWER

1. Why did Jesus curse the fig tree? _____
_____
_____

2. What did Jesus say the disciples could do if they had faith? _____

3. In the Parable of the Two Sons, Jesus said that who believed before the priests and the elders believed?
_____

4. In the Parable of the Wicked Vinedressers, the vine-dressers killed whom? _____

**5.** Who thought this parable was about themselves?

_____

**6.** What was their reaction to this parable? _____

_____

**7.** In the Parable of the Wedding Feast, who hosts the wedding? _____

**8.** What is the king's reaction to his servants' deaths?

_____

_____

## UNSCRAMBLE THE (parables)

1. Wesor
2. Tusmard Dese
3. Tols Eshpe
4. Siwe dan Ofosilh Givirns
5. Dogo Masriatna
6. Lots Nico
7. Chir Lofo
8. Lantets
9. Degiwdn Eafst
10. Remnuifcul Verastn

ANSWERS p. 149

## MATCHING

1. Lamp Under a Basket

2. The Marriage

3. Patched Garment

4. Leaven

5. Pearl of Great Price

6. Wedding Garment

a. Chief priests and Pharisees

b. Pharisees and Scribes

c. Pharisees and Disciples of John

d. Multitudes concerning John the Baptist

e. Disciples on the Mount of Olives

f. Disciples

**7.** Wise and Foolish Virgins

g. Multitude on the Seashore

**8.** Lost Coin

**9.** Persistent Widow

ANSWERS
p. 150

**10.** Children in the Marketplace

## FILL IN THE BLANKS

1. The Parable of the Fig Tree illustrates how to recognize the _____ _____ _____.

2. The kingdom of heaven will be like ten _____, five of whom are _____ and five are _____.

3. The Parable of the Wise and Foolish Virgins is an illustration of what will happen at _____ _____ _____ _____ _____ _____ _____.

4. In the Parable of the _____, the master congratulated the _____ and _____ servants by saying, "Enter into the joy of your lord."

**5.** The unprofitable servant in the Parable of the _____ will be cast into the _____ _____ where there will be _____ and _____ of teeth.

**6.** The first parable in the book of Mark is the Parable of the _____, and it comes right after Jesus' _____ and _____ send for him.

**7.** Jesus said, "Is a _____ to be put under a _____ or under a bed? . . . There is nothing _____ which will not be _____."

**8.** The Parable of the Growing Seed says, "The _____ of God is as if a man should scatter _____ on the ground, and should sleep by _____ and rise by _____, and the _____ should sprout and grow."

---

Q. Why did the disciples run out of the field where Jesus was speaking?
A. Because they saw a pair of bulls!

---

## WORD BANK

day    victors    hidden

new earth    virgins    kingdom

night    brothers    outer darkness

basket    cents    seed    end times

talents    lamp    revealed    weekend

mother    singing    sower    sister

wise    hidden

the coming of the Son of Man

foolish    faithful    good    brother

## MULTIPLE CHOICE

1. **Jesus did not speak to the people without what, according to Mark 4:34?**
   A. moral lessons
   B. parables
   C. his lawyer present
   D. his disciples listening and learning

2. **Jesus, in speaking to the disciples about salt, said everyone will be seasoned with:**

# Top Ten Parables That Didn't Make It

10. Parable of the Lost Man (who wouldn't ask for directions)

9. Parable of the Drunkards in the Vineyard

8. Parable of the Sewer

7. Parable of the Good Politician

6. Parable of the Lost Jeep

5. Parable of the Talent Agent

4. Parable of the Hairnet

3. Parable of the Fig Newton

2. Parable of the Unmerciful Detergent

1. Parable of the Mustard Stain

**A.** trials
**B.** paprika
**C.** fire
**D.** salt

3. **When people brought their little children to see Jesus, the disciples:**
   **A.** rebuked them
   **B.** welcomed them
   **C.** taught them
   **D.** babysat them

4. **Who gave more to the church than all the rich who had contributed to the treasury?**
   **A.** the Pharisees
   **B.** Zacchaeus
   **C.** Bill Gates
   **D.** the widow with two mites

5. **The fig tree's leaves will wither away unlike:**
   **A.** Dick Clark's physical appearance
   **B.** the Word of God
   **C.** the Temple of God
   **D.** the heavens and the earth

6. **What topic was Jesus discussing with the teachers in the temple as a child when his parents found him there?**
   **A.** we don't know
   **B.** interpretations of the Torah

C. whether or not they would change his grade
   from a B+ to an A
D. the laws regarding the Jewish diet

7. **The story in which the wise man built his house
   upon the rock is a lesson about:**
   A. carpentry
   B. faith
   C. hypocrisy
   D. predestination

8. **In the Parable of the Sower, the seed that was
   sown by the wayside:**
   A. was choked by rocks
   B. was eaten by hairy cows
   C. grew into a giant beanstalk
   D. was trampled and eaten by birds

**TALL TALE**

One day a _____ was walking with two
___NOUN___

friends when it approached a _____ in the
___NOUN___

road. It _____, "Oh my stars! I've just
___VERB (PAST TENSE)___

seen a _____ _____! I can't believe it!" So,
___ADJECTIVE___ ___NOUN___

the two friends and it _____
___VERB (PAST TENSE)___

the _____ and put it in their
___NOUN___

_____. They invited all their other
___ROOM OF HOUSE___

friends over to _____ it. But one friend did not
___VERB___

think this exploitation was right—he confronted his friends.

"You should not be so _____
___CHARACTER TRAIT___

with this that you have discovered!" His friends listened to

him and _____. So, they let
___VERB (PAST TENSE)___

the _____ go back to where it had come
___NOUN___

from, and they all lived in _____ from
___IDEAL SETTING___

then on.

Moral: _____.
___MORAL___

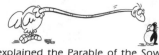

1. When Jesus explained the Parable of the Sower, what happened to those whose seed was sown onto the rocks? _____

2. Those whose seed fell on the good ground do what? _____

3. What is the point of the Parable of the Revealed Light? _____

4. The Parable of the Good Samaritan only appears in which gospel? _____

5. Who tested Jesus, that he told the Parable of the Good Samaritan? _____

6. What did the Samaritan do for the wounded man?

   _____

7. Why did Jesus tell the Parable of the Rich Fool?

   _____

   _____

8. What happened to the Rich Fool when he had an overabundance of crops that he desired to keep for the years to come? _____

# ANSWERS TO:
# TELL ME A STORY

## FILL IN THE BLANKS

| # ANSWER | REFERENCE |
|----------|-----------|
| 1. Sower | Matthew 13 |
| 2. by the wayside, in stony places, among thorns, on good ground | Matthew 13 |
| 3. seeing, see, hearing, hear | Matthew 13 |
| 4. disciples, blessed | Matthew 13 |
| 5. heaven, man, good, slept, tares | Matthew 13 |
| 6. burned, barn | Matthew 13 |
| 7. mustard, nest | Matthew 13 |
| 8. leaven, meal, leavened | Matthew 13 |

## TRUE OR FALSE

| # ANSWER | REFERENCE |
|----------|-----------|
| 1. False—he did explain | Matthew 13 |
| 2. True | Matthew 13, Psalm 78:2 |
| 3. False—only the disciples | Matthew 13 |

## TRUE OR FALSE—cont'd

| # ANSWER | REFERENCE |
|----------|-----------|
| 4. True | Matthew 13 |
| 5. True | Matthew 13 |
| 6. False | |
| 7. False—angels will | Matthew 13 |
| 8. True | Matthew 13 |
| 9. True | Matthew 13 |
| 10. True | Matthew 18 |

## MULTIPLE CHOICE

| # ANSWER | REFERENCE |
|----------|-----------|
| 1. a | Matthew 18 |
| 2. b | Matthew 18 |
| 3. d | Matthew 18 |
| 4. c | Matthew 18 |
| 5. b | Matthew 19 |
| 6. a | Matthew 20 |
| 7. c | Matthew 20 |
| 8. d | Matthew 20 |

## SHORT ANSWER

| # | ANSWER | REFERENCE |
|---|--------|-----------|
| 1. | because nothing grew on it but leaves | Matthew 21 |
| 2. | move a mountain into the sea | Matthew 21 |
| 3. | tax collectors and harlots | Matthew 21 |
| 4. | servants and the owner's son | Matthew 21 |
| 5. | chief priests and Pharisees | Matthew 21 |
| 6. | wanted to lay hands on him but feared the people | Matthew 21 |
| 7. | the King, for his son | Matthew 22 |
| 8. | sent out armies and burned the cities, then invited strangers | Matthew 22 |

## UNSCRAMBLE

| # | ANSWER |
|---|--------|
| 1. | Sower |
| 2. | Mustard Seed |
| 3. | Lost Sheep |

## UNSCRAMBLE—cont'd

| # ANSWER |
| --- |
| 4. Wise and Foolish Virgins |
| 5. Good Samaritan |
| 6. Lost Coin |
| 7. Rich Fool |
| 8. Talents |
| 9. Wedding Feast |
| 10. Unmerciful Servant |

## MATCHING

| # ANSWER | REFERENCE |
| --- | --- |
| 1. f | Mark 4 |
| 2. c | Matthew 9 |
| 3. c | Mark 2 |
| 4. g | Matthew 13 |
| 5. f | Matthew 13 |
| 6. a | Matthew 22 |
| 7. e | Matthew 25 |
| 8. b | Luke 15 |
| 9. f | Luke 18 |
| 10. d | Luke 7 |

# FILL IN THE BLANKS

| # | ANSWER | REFERENCE |
|---|--------|-----------|
| 1. | the end times | Matthew 24 |
| 2. | virgins, wise, foolish | Matthew 25 |
| 3. | the coming of the Son of Man | Matthew 25 |
| 4. | talents, good, faithful | Matthew 25 |
| 5. | talents, outer darkness, weeping, gnashing | Matthew 25 |
| 6. | sower, mother, brothers | Mark 4 |
| 7. | lamp, basket, hidden, revealed | Mark 4 |
| 8. | kingdom, seed, night, day, seed | Mark 4 |

# MULTIPLE CHOICE

| # | ANSWER | REFERENCE |
|---|--------|-----------|
| 1. | b | Mark 4:34 |
| 2. | c | Mark 9:50 |
| 3. | a | Mark 10:13 |
| 4. | d | Mark 12:43 |
| 5. | b | Mark 13:28 |
| 6. | a | Luke 2 |

| # ANSWER | REFERENCE |
|---|---|
| 7. c | Luke 6 |
| 8. d | Luke 8 |

## SHORT
## ANSWER

| # ANSWER | REFERENCE |
|---|---|
| 1. have no root and in time of temptation fall away | Luke 8 |
| 2. keep it and bear fruit with patience | Luke 8 |
| 3. to whoever has, more will be given; whoever does not have, even what he seems to have will be taken away | Luke 8 |
| 4. Luke | Luke 10 |
| 5. a lawyer | Luke 10 |
| 6. bandaged his wounds, poured oil and wine on him, had him taken care of at an inn | Luke 10 |
| 7. a man in the crowd demanded that Jesus tell his brother to divide an inheritance between the two | Luke 12 |
| 8. he died | Luke 12 |

# TEACHINGS AND
# ILLUSTRATIONS OF CHRIST

# What Just Happened?

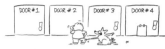

1. **Which of the following occurred as a result of Adam and Eve's sin?**
   **A.** They experienced knowledge of evil.
   **B.** They experienced shame and guilt.
   **C.** They feared God's presence.
   **D.** all of the above
   **E.** The shekel market fell 200 points.

ANSWERS
p. 183

2. **What happened immediately after Adam and Eve made clothes for themselves?**
   **A.** They went out of the garden.
   **B.** They heard God walking in the garden.
   **C.** They went out of style.
   **D.** They hid in the trees.

3. **God sent The Flood to cover the earth because:**
   **A.** The wickedness of man was great in the earth, and all his thoughts were evil.
   **B.** The people of Ur hated God.
   **C.** The people of the earth laughed in the face of his warnings.
   **D.** Simon said to.

4. **How long did The Flood cover the earth?**
   **A.** 2 years
   **B.** too long
   **C.** 5 months
   **D.** 40 days

1. The tower of Babel was built to do what?

   _____

2. How did God punish the men who built the tower?

   _____

3. What event sparked God's destruction of Sodom?

   _____

   _____

4. Who pulled Lot out of the city of Sodom?

   _____

   _____

## MATCHING

1. Abraham
2. Samson
3. Ruth
4. David
5. Lot
6. Nehemiah
7. Bill and Ted
8. Hosea
9. Rahab
10. Esther

a. escaped burning city with wife and daughters
b. hid spies in her home
c. rebuilt a city wall
d. was asked to sacrifice his son
e. had an excellent adventure
f. won a beauty pagent
g. destroyed a house full of Philistines
h. married a prostitute
i. murdered a soldier
j. met her husband while working in the fields

## FILL IN THE BLANKS

1. Rahab lived in _____.

2. Ehud killed this king: _____.

ANSWERS p. 184

3. _____ had Uriah killed.

4. This city was raided by Israel: _____.

5. Ruth's first mother-in-law was _____.

6. The Philistines stole this important item from the Israelites: _____.

7. This man ran from God to Tarshish: _____.

8. Lot's wife turned into _____.

**WORD BANK**

| Naomi | Ark | Sand | Eglon |
|-------|-----|------|-------|
| Jonah | Bezek | Salt | Salt |
| Jericho | David | Danny | Rahab |

**PUT THE FOLLOWING IN ORDER**

**Plagues**

1. Flies
2. Livestock died
3. Darkness over the land
4. Water turned to blood
5. Hail storm
6. Frogs
7. Locusts

8. Boils

9. Death of the first born

10. Lice

## Ten Commandments

1. Remember the Sabbath Day and keep it holy

2. Do not commit adultery

3. Have no other gods before Me

4. Do not covet

ANSWERS p. 185

5. Honor your father and mother

6. Have no graven images

7. Do not murder

8. Do not lie

9. Do not take God's name in vain

10. Do not steal

---

# HOW ABOUT THAT!

A man claimed he saw Noah's ark on Mt. Ararat in 1908, and today a picture of it exists.

---

1. Passover commemorates Israel's deliverance from Egypt and is a reminder that Christ spared the first born.

2. The Feast of Unleavened Bread is symbolized by communion in modern days.

3. The Day of Firstfruits dedicated the firstfruits of the wheat harvest.

4. The Feast of Pentecost, Harvest, and Weeks is symbolized by the outpouring of the Holy Spirit.

5. The Day of Trumpets commemorates Israel's defeat of Jericho.

6. The Day of Atonement is fulfilled in Christ's crucifixion.

7. The Feast of Tabernacles commemorates God's deliverance.

8. The Feast of Purim was held to recognize the goodness God bestowed on his people because of their sacrifices.

## FILL IN THE BLANKS

1. Because Sarai lived in Pharaoh's house claiming to be Abram's sister, God sent _____ on Pharaoh's house.

2. What did Joseph's brothers find in their sacks of grain? _____

3. The people of Israel plundered the Egyptians by having every woman ask her neighbor for articles of _____ and _____ and _____.

4. Pharaoh's magicians could imitate _____ of Moses' miracles.

**5.** Why did the Israelites call the food sent to them in the desert manna? _____

**6.** Moses burned the golden calf, ground it into powder, poured it on the water and made the Israelites _____ _____.

ANSWERS p. 186

## WORD BANK

> Because it means "what is it?"
>
> locusts    two    drink it
>
> none    copper    his own money
>
> silver    gold    worms    clothing
>
> Because it was white    plagues

**MULTIPLE CHOICE**

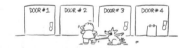

1. **Moses did what to part the Red Sea?**
   **A.** commanded the waters to part
   **B.** hit it with a rod
   **C.** sang "Pharaoh, Pharaoh, whoa, oh, Let my people go!"
   **D.** lifted up a rod and stretched out his hand

# Top Ten Feasts the Israelites Didn't Celebrate

10. Feast of Juicyfruits

9. Combover

8. Feast of Tubas

7. Feast of Harems

6. Feast of Winnebagos

5. Feast of day-old doughnuts

4. Feast of Garlic Bread

3. Day of Ham

2. Day of Organ Donors

1. Wash A Sauna

2. **How many people exited Egypt with Moses?**
   **A.** six hundred men with their families
   **B.** six thousand men with their families
   **C.** six hundred thousand men with their families
   **D.** none

3. **Where was the Promised Land?**
   **A.** the mountains of the Amorites all the way to the land of the Canaanites and Lebanon as far as the river Euphrates
   **B.** the mountains of the Amorites all the way to the land of the Canaanites but not beyond, for that is the land of the pagan peoples
   **C.** the great Smokey Mountains, all the way to the Adirondacks of New England
   **D.** all the land of the Canaanites, and no more

4. **What flowed in the Promised Land?**
   **A.** milk
   **B.** honey
   **C.** hair
   **D.** manna

5. **Which of the spies who entered Canaan thought the Israelites should enter?**
   **A.** Moses and Aaron
   **B.** Joshua and Caleb
   **C.** Rocky and Bullwinkle
   **D.** Reuben and Igal

6. **Why did the Israelites go to war with the Benjaminites?**

**A.** They kept raising the price of oil

**B.** They pillaged the Israelite's land

**C.** A Levite's concubine was raped

**D.** They stole the ark of the covenant

### 7. What was Samson's riddle about?

**A.** a lion

**B.** a bear

**C.** I don't know, but it brought the house down.

**D.** a Philistine

### 8. Which of the following were Delilah's attempts to weaken Samson?

**A.** bound him with fresh bowstrings

**B.** tied him with weathered ropes

**C.** wove five locks of his hair

**D.** took away his Nautilus system

ANSWERS
p. 187

## TRUE OR FALSE

1. David put only one stone in his bag when he prepared to fight Goliath.

2. Saul gave his daughter Michal to another man while she was still married to David.

3. A medium brought Samuel back from the dead to speak to Saul.

4. David built a temple.

5. Assyria captured the northern kingdom of Israel.

6. Both Elijah and Elisha raised boys from the dead.

7. The first thing the Israelites built when returning from captivity in Babylon was a new temple.

8. Israel wanted a king so that they could be like other nations and fight.

9. Solomon had a hard time getting dates.

10. Jonah stayed in the fish for forty days and nights.

**MULTIPLE CHOICE**

1. **The wise men saw the star how many times?**
   A. one
   B. two
   C. infinity
   D. four

2. **How did Joseph know that God did not want him to take Jesus back to Judea when the family returned from Egypt?**
   A. dream
   B. Mary knew
   C. when he tried to go, his feet caught on fire
   D. finger writing on the wall

3. **Who saw the Holy Spirit descend on Jesus like a dove?**
   A. Jesus
   B. all who had eyes to see

**C.** Jesus and John the Baptist

**D.** members of the local birdwatchers society

4. **The centurion said to Jesus:**
   **A.** ''Only speak a word, and my servant will be healed.''
   **B.** ''Please, come and heal my servant.''
   **C.** ''You complete me.''
   **D.** ''Your will be done.''

5. **What name completes this prophecy: ''Out of _____ I called my Son.''**
   **A.** Mary
   **B.** Bethlehem
   **C.** Africa
   **D.** Egypt

ANSWERS
p. 188

6. **What was Jesus doing when the tempest arose around the boat?**
   **A.** preaching
   **B.** eating
   **C.** sleeping
   **D.** knitting

7. **What interrupted Jesus on his way to heal Jairus's daughter?**

---

**Q.** What was the first thing Adam and Eve did when they were kicked out of the Garden of Eden?

**A.** Raised Cain!

---

**A.** a hemorrhaging woman
**B.** a demon-possessed man
**C.** Tom Brokaw with a special news report
**D.** a centurion

8. **Whose Son did the two blind men who were following Jesus say that He was?**
   **A.** God's
   **B.** David's
   **C.** Joseph's
   **D.** Daniel-son

## UNSCRAMBLE

1. Gansirfatruniot
2. Recrusretnoi
3. Lumacteima Peretonic
4. Ficurxnioci
5. Salt Puresp
6. Tesoctnep
7. Siarminoys Njoruyes
8. Lapu febreo het Hendrsani
9. Toscdowok
10. Dingdwe Puesrp fo het Ambl

ANSWERS
p. 189

Q. Who was the best high-jumper in the Bible?
A. Jesus, He cleared the temple.

# ANSWERS TO:
# WHAT JUST HAPPENED?

## MULTIPLE CHOICE

| # ANSWER | REFERENCE |
|----------|-----------|
| 1. d | Genesis 3:7–8 |
| 2. b | Genesis 3:8 |
| 3. a | Genesis 6:5 |
| 4. c | Genesis 7:11–8:4 |

## SHORT ANSWER

| # ANSWER | REFERENCE |
|----------|-----------|
| 1. to make a name for themselves | Genesis 11:4 |
| 2. confused their language | Genesis 11:8 |
| 3. the men of the city desired to rape the angels staying in Lot's home | Genesis 19:1–11 |
| 4. the angels pulled Lot, his wife and two daughters out | Genesis 19:16 |

## MATCHING

| # ANSWER | REFERENCE |
|----------|-----------|
| 1. d | Genesis 22 |
| 2. g | Judges 16 |
| 3. j | Ruth 2 |
| 4. i | 2 Samuel 11 |
| 5. a | Genesis 19 |
| 6. c | Nehemiah 3 |
| 7. e | (movie) |
| 8. h | Hosea 1 |
| 9. b | Joshua 2 |
| 10. f | Esther 2 |

## FILL IN THE BLANKS

| # ANSWER | REFERENCE |
|----------|-----------|
| 1. Jericho | Joshua 2 |
| 2. Eglon | Judges 3 |
| 3. David | 2 Samuel 11 |
| 4. Bezek | Judges 1 |
| 5. Naomi | Ruth 1 |
| 6. Ark | 1 Samuel 5 |

| # ANSWER | REFERENCE |
|----------|-----------|
| 7. Jonah | Jonah 1 |
| 8. Salt | Genesis 19:26 |

## PUT THE FOLLOWING IN ORDER

| # ANSWER | REFERENCE |
|----------|-----------|
| 1. Plagues: 4, 6, 10, 1, 2, 8, 5, 7, 3, 9 | Exodus 7–12 |
| 2. 10 Commandments: 3, 6, 9, 1, 5, 7, 2, 10, 8, 4 | Exodus 20 |

## TRUE OR FALSE

| # ANSWER | REFERENCE |
|----------|-----------|
| 1. True | Exodus 12:27 |
| 2. False; True Church | John 6, 1 Cor. 5 |
| 3. False; Barley | Leviticus 23 |
| 4. True | Exodus 23, Lev. 23, Num. 28, Deut. 16, Acts 2 |

## TRUE OR FALSE—cont'd

| # ANSWER | REFERENCE |
|----------|-----------|
| 5. False; consecrates | Leviticus 23, Num. 10 |
| 6. True | Hebrews 9 |
| 7. True | Leviticus 23 |
| 8. False; to recognize Deliverence from genocide during Esther's time | Esther 9 |

## FILL IN THE BLANKS

| # ANSWER | REFERENCE |
|----------|-----------|
| 1. plagues | Genesis 12:7 |
| 2. his own money | Genesis 42:35 |
| 3. silver, gold, and clothing | Exodus 3:22 |
| 4. three | Exodus 7:11, 8:7, 22 |
| 5. what is it? | Exodus 16:15 |
| 6. drink it | Exodus 32:20 |

## MULTIPLE CHOICE

| # ANSWER | REFERENCE |
| --- | --- |
| 1. d | Exodus 14:16 |
| 2. c | Exodus 12:37 |
| 3. a | Deuteronomy 1:5–8 |
| 4. a,b | Exodus 3:8 |
| 5. b | Numbers 14 |
| 6. c | Judges 20 |
| 7. a | Judges 14 |
| 8. a | Judges 16 |

## TRUE OR FALSE

| # ANSWER | REFERENCE |
| --- | --- |
| 1. False; five | 1 Samuel 17:40 |
| 2. True | 1 Samuel 25:44 |
| 3. True | 1 Samuel 28:11–19 |
| 4. False | 2 Samuel 7:1–7 |
| 5. True | 2 Kings 17:5–6 |
| 6. True | 2 Kings 4, 1 Kings 17 |

## TRUE OR FALSE—cont'd

| # ANSWER | REFERENCE |
|----------|-----------|
| 7. False; altar | Ezra 3:2 |
| 8. True | 1 Samuel 8:20 |
| 9. False | |
| 10. False; three days and nights | Jonah 1:17 |

## MULTIPLE CHOICE

| # ANSWER | REFERENCE |
|----------|-----------|
| 1. b | Matthew 2:2, 9 |
| 2. a | Matthew 2:12 |
| 3. c | Matthew 3:16, John 1:32 |
| 4. a | Matthew 8:8 |
| 5. d | Matthew 2:15 |
| 6. c | Matthew 8:24 |
| 7. a | Matthew 9:20 |
| 8. b | Matthew 9:27 |

## UNSCRAMBLE

| # | ANSWER |
|---|--------|
| 1. | Transfiguration |
| 2. | Resurrection |
| 3. | Immaculate Reception |
| 4. | Crucifixion |
| 5. | Last Supper |
| 6. | Pentecost |
| 7. | Missionary Journeys |
| 8. | Paul before the Sanhedrin |
| 9. | Woodstock |
| 10. | Wedding Supper of the Lamb |

# PROPHECIES OF THE MESSIAH FULFILLED IN JESUS CHRIST

*Presented Here in Their Order of Fulfillment*

## SEED OF A WOMAN

**Prophecy**   Genesis 3:15
"And I will put enmity between you and the woman, and between your seed and her Seed; He shall bruise your head, and you shall bruise His heel."

**Fulfilled**   Galatians 4:4
But when the fullness of the time had come, God sent forth His Son, born of a woman, born under the law.

## SEED OF ABRAHAM

**Prophecy**   Genesis 12:3
"I will bless those who bless you, and I will curse him who curses you; and in you all the families of the earth shall be blessed."

**Fulfilled**   Matthew 1:1
The book of the genealogy of Jesus Christ, the Son of David, the Son of Abraham.

## SEED OF ISAAC

**Prophecy**   Genesis 17:19
Then God said: "No, Sarah your wife shall bear you a son, and you shall call his name Isaac; I will establish My covenant with him for an everlasting covenant, *and* with his descendants after him."

**Fulfilled**    Luke 3:34
*The son* of Jacob, *the son* of Isaac, *the son* of Abraham, *the son* of Terah, *the son* of Nahor.


## SEED OF JACOB

**Prophecy**    Numbers 24:17
"I see Him, but not now; I behold Him, but not near; a Star shall come out of Jacob; a Scepter shall rise out of Israel, and batter the brow of Moab, and destroy all the sons of tumult."

**Fulfilled**    Matthew 1:2
Abraham begot Isaac, Isaac begot Jacob, and Jacob begot Judah and his brothers.


## FROM THE TRIBE OF JUDAH

**Prophecy**    Genesis 49:10
"The scepter shall not depart from Judah, nor a lawgiver from between his feet, until Shiloh comes; and to Him *shall be* the obedience of the people."

**Fulfilled**    Luke 3:33
*The son* of Amminadab, *the son* of Ram, *the son* of Hezron, *the son* of Perez, *the son* of Judah.


## HEIR TO THE THRONE OF DAVID

**Prophecy**    Isaiah 9:7
Of the increase of *His* government and peace *there will be* no end, upon the throne of David and over His kingdom, to order it and establish it with judgment and justice from that time forward, even forever. The zeal of the Lord of hosts will perform this.

**Fulfilled**    Luke 1:32, 33

"He will be great, and will be called the Son of the Highest; and the Lord God will give Him the throne of His father David.

"And He will reign over the house of Jacob forever, and of His kingdom there will be no end."


## BORN IN BETHLEHEM

**Prophecy**    Micah 5:2

"But you, Bethlehem Ephrathah, *though* you are little among the thousands of Judah, *yet* out of you shall come forth to Me the One to be ruler in Israel, whose goings forth *have been* from of old, from everlasting."

**Fulfilled**    Luke 2:4, 5, 7

And Joseph also went up from Galilee, out of the city of Nazareth, into Judea, to the city of David, which is called Bethlehem, because he was of the house and lineage of David, to be registered with Mary, his betrothed wife, who was with child.

And she brought forth her firstborn Son, and wrapped Him in swaddling cloths, and laid Him in a manger, because there was no room for them in the inn.


## TIME FOR HIS BAPTISM

**Prophecy**    Daniel 9:25

"Know therefore and understand, *that* from the going forth of the command to restore and build Jerusalem until Messiah the Prince, *there shall be* seven weeks and sixty-two weeks; the street shall be built again, and the wall, even in troublesome times."

**Fulfilled**    Luke 3:21, 22

Now when all the people were baptized, it came to pass that Jesus also was baptized; and while He prayed, the heaven was opened.

And the Holy Spirit descended in bodily form like a dove

upon Him, and a voice came from heaven which said, "You are My beloved Son; in You I am well pleased."

## TO BE BORN OF A VIRGIN

**Prophecy**   Isaiah 7:14
"Therefore the Lord Himself will give you a sign: Behold, the virgin shall conceive and bear a Son, and shall call His name Immanuel."

**Fulfilled**   Luke 1:26, 27, 30, 31
Now in the sixth month the angel Gabriel was sent by God to a city of Galilee named Nazareth, to a virgin betrothed to a man whose name was Joseph, of the house of David. The virgin's name *was* Mary.

Then the angel said to her, "Do not be afraid, Mary, for you have found favor with God.

"And behold, you will conceive in your womb and bring forth a Son, and shall call His name Jesus."

## SLAUGHTER OF THE INNOCENTS

**Prophecy**   Jeremiah 31:15
Thus says the Lord: "A voice was heard in Ramah, lamentation *and* bitter weeping, Rachel weeping for her children, refusing to be comforted for her children, because they *are* no more."

**Fulfilled**   Matthew 2:16–18
Then Herod, when he saw that he was deceived by the wise men, was exceedingly angry; and he sent forth and put to death all the male children who were in Bethlehem and in all its districts, from two years old and under, according to the time which he had determined from the wise men.

Then was fulfilled what was spoken by Jeremiah the prophet, saying:

"A voice was heard in Ramah, lamentation, weeping, and

*great mourning, Rachel weeping for her children, refusing to be comforted, because they were no more."*

## FLIGHT TO EGYPT

**Prophecy**  Hosea 11:1
"When Israel *was* a child, I loved him, and out of Egypt I called My son."

**Fulfilled**  Matthew 2:14, 15
When he arose, he took the young Child and His mother by night and departed for Egypt, and was there until the death of Herod, that it might be fulfilled which was spoken by the Lord through the prophet, saying, *"Out of Egypt I called My Son."*

## PRECEDED BY A FORERUNNER

**Prophecy**  Malachi 3:1
"Behold, I send My messenger, and he will prepare the way before Me. And the Lord, whom you seek, will suddenly come to His temple, even the Messenger of the covenant, in whom you delight. Behold, He is coming," says the LORD of hosts.

**Fulfilled**  Luke 7:24, 27
When the messengers of John had departed, He began to speak to the multitudes concerning John: "What did you go out into the wilderness to see? A reed shaken by the wind?

"This is *he* of whom it is written: *'Behold, I send My messenger before Your face, who will prepare Your way before You.'*

## DECLARED THE SON OF GOD

**Prophecy**  Psalm 2:7
"I will declare the decree: the LORD has said to Me, 'You *are* My Son, today I have begotten You.'"

**Fulfilled**   Matthew 3:17
And suddenly a voice *came* from heaven, saying, "This is My beloved Son, in whom I am well pleased."

## GALILEAN MINISTRY

**Prophecy**   Isaiah 9:1, 2
Nevertheless the gloom *will* not *be* upon her who *is* distressed, as when at first He lightly esteemed the land of Zebulun and the land of Naphtali, and afterward more heavily oppressed *her, by* the way of the sea, beyond the Jordan, in Galilee of the Gentiles.

The people who walked in darkness have seen a great light; those who dwelt in the land of the shadow of death, upon them a light has shined.

**Fulfilled**   Matthew 4:13–16
And leaving Nazareth, He came and dwelt in Capernaum, which is by the sea, in the regions of Zebulun and Naphtali, that it might be fulfilled which was spoken by Isaiah the prophet, saying:

"The land of Zebulun and the land of Naphtali, the way of the sea, beyond the Jordan, Galilee of the Gentiles: the people who sat in darkness saw a great light, And upon those who sat in the region and shadow of death light has dawned."

## A PROPHET

**Prophecy**   Deuteronomy 18:15
"The LORD your God will raise up for you a Prophet like me from your midst, from your brethren. Him you shall hear."

**Fulfilled**   Acts 3:20, 22
"And that He may send Jesus Christ, who was preached to you before.

"For Moses truly said to the fathers, 'The LORD *your God*

*will raise up for you a Prophet like me from your brethren.*
*Him you shall hear in all things, whatever He says to you."'*

## TO HEAL THE BROKENHEARTED

**Prophecy**   Isaiah 61:1, 2
"The Spirit of the Lord GOD *is* upon Me, because the LORD
has anointed Me to preach good tidings to the poor; He has
sent Me to heal the brokenhearted, to proclaim liberty to the
captives, and the opening of the prison to *those who are*
bound; to proclaim the acceptable year of the LORD, and the
day of vengeance of our God; to comfort all who mourn."

**Fulfilled**   Luke 4:18, 19
*"The Spirit of the LORD is upon Me, because He has anointed*
*Me to preach the gospel to the poor. He has sent Me to heal*
*the brokenhearted, to preach deliverance to the captives and*
*recovery of sight to the blind, to set at liberty those who are*
*oppressed, to preach the acceptable year of the LORD."*

## REJECTED BY HIS OWN PEOPLE, THE JEWS

**Prophecy**   Isaiah 53:3
He is despised and rejected by men, a man of sorrows and
acquainted with grief. And we hid, as it were, *our* faces from
Him; He was despised, and we did not esteem Him.

**Fulfilled**   John 1:11
He came to His own, and His own did not receive Him.

    Luke 23:18
And they all cried out at once, saying, "Away with this *Man,*
and release to us Barabbas."

## PRIEST AFTER ORDER OF MELCHIZEDEK

**Prophecy**   Psalm 110:4
The LORD has sworn and will not relent, "You *are* a priest
forever according to the order of Melchizedek."

**Fulfilled**    Hebrews 5:5, 6

So also Christ did not glorify Himself to become High Priest, *but it* was He who said to Him: *"You are My Son, today I have begotten You."*

As He also *says* in another *place: "You are a priest forever according to the order of Melchizedek."*


## TRIUMPHAL ENTRY

**Prophecy**    Zechariah 9:9

"Rejoice greatly, O daughter of Zion! Shout, O daughter of Jerusalem! Behold, your King is coming to you; He *is* just and having salvation, lowly and riding on a donkey, a colt, the foal of a donkey."

**Fulfilled**    Mark 11:7, 9, 11

Then they brought the colt to Jesus and threw their garments on it, and He sat on it.

Then those who went before and those who followed cried out, saying: "Hosanna! *'Blessed is He who comes in the name of the* LORD!'"

And Jesus went into Jerusalem and into the temple. So when He had looked around at all things, as the hour was already late, He went out to Bethany with the twelve.


## BETRAYED BY A FRIEND

**Prophecy**    Psalm 41:9

Even my own familiar friend in whom I trusted, who ate my bread, has lifted up *his* heel against me.

**Fulfilled**    Luke 22:47, 48

And while He was still speaking, behold, a multitude; and he who was called Judas, one of the twelve, went before them and drew near to Jesus to kiss Him.

But Jesus said to him, "Judas, are you betraying the Son of Man with a kiss?"

## SOLD FOR THIRTY PIECES OF SILVER

**Prophecy**   Zechariah 11:12
Then I said to them, "If it is agreeable to you, give *me* my wages; and if not, refrain." So they weighed out for my wages thirty *pieces* of silver.

**Fulfilled**   Matthew 26:15
And said, "What are you willing to give me if I deliver Him to you?" And they counted out to him thirty pieces of silver.


## ACCUSED BY FALSE WITNESSES

**Prophecy**   Psalm 35:11
Fierce witnesses rise up; they ask me *things* that I do not know.

**Fulfilled**   Mark 14:57, 58
   And some rose up and bore false witness against Him, saying, "We heard Him say, 'I will destroy this temple that *is* made with hands, and within three days I will build another made without hands.'"


## SILENT TO ACCUSATIONS

**Prophecy**   Isaiah 53:7
He was oppressed and He was afflicted, yet He opened not His mouth; He was led as a lamb to the slaughter, and as a sheep before its shearers is silent, so He opened not His mouth.

**Fulfilled**   Mark 15:4, 5
Then Pilate asked Him again, saying, "Do You answer nothing? See how many things they testify against You!"
   But Jesus still answered nothing, so that Pilate marveled.

## SPAT UPON AND SMITTEN

**Prophecy**   Isaiah 50:6
I gave My back to those who struck *Me*, and My cheeks to those who plucked out the beard; I did not hide My face from shame and spitting.

**Fulfilled**   Matthew 26:67
Then they spat in His face and beat Him; and others struck *Him* with the palms of their hands.


## HATED WITHOUT REASON

**Prophecy**   Psalm 35:19
Let them not rejoice over me who are wrongfully my enemies; Nor let them wink with the eye who hate me without a cause.

**Fulfilled**   John 15:24, 25
"If I had not done among them the works which no one else did, they would have no sin; but now they have seen and also hated both Me and My Father.

"But *this happened* that the word might be fulfilled which is written in their law, *'They hated Me without a cause.'"*


## VICARIOUS SACRIFICE

**Prophecy**   Isaiah 53:5
But He *was* wounded for our transgressions, *He was* bruised for our iniquities; the chastisement for our peace *was* upon Him, and by His stripes we are healed.

**Fulfilled**   Romans 5:6, 8
For when we were still without strength, in due time Christ died for the ungodly.

But God demonstrates His own love toward us, in that while we were still sinners, Christ died for us.

## CRUCIFIED WITH MALEFACTORS

**Prophecy**   Isaiah 53:12
Therefore I will divide Him a portion with the great, and He shall divide the spoil with the strong, because He poured out His soul unto death, and He was numbered with the transgressors, and He bore the sin of many, And made intercession for the transgressors.

**Fulfilled**   Mark 15:27, 28
With Him they also crucified two robbers, one on His right and the other on His left.

So the Scripture was fulfilled which says, "And He was numbered with the transgressors."

## PIERCED THROUGH HANDS AND FEET

**Prophecy**   Zechariah 12:10
"And I will pour on the house of David and on the inhabitants of Jerusalem the Spirit of grace and supplication; then they will look on Me whom they have pierced; they will mourn for Him as one mourns for *his* only *son,* and grieve for Him as one grieves for a firstborn."

**Fulfilled**   John 20:27
Then He said to Thomas, "Reach your finger here, and look at My hands; and reach your hand *here,* and put *it* into My side. Do not be unbelieving, but believing."

## SCORNED AND MOCKED

**Prophecy**   Psalm 22:7, 8
All those who see Me laugh Me to scorn; they shoot out the lip, they shake the head, *saying,* "He trusted in the LORD, let Him rescue Him; let Him deliver Him, since He delights in Him!"

**Fulfilled**    Luke 23:35

And the people stood looking on. But even the rulers with them sneered, saying, "He saved others; let Him save Himself if He is the Christ, the chosen of God."


## GIVEN VINEGAR AND GALL

**Prophecy**    Psalm 69:21

They also gave me gall for my food, and for my thirst they gave me vinegar to drink.

**Fulfilled**    Matthew 27:34

They gave Him sour wine mingled with gall to drink. But when He had tasted *it,* He would not drink.


## PRAYER FOR HIS ENEMIES

**Prophecy**    Psalm 109:4

In return for my love they are my accusers, but I *give myself to* prayer.

**Fulfilled**    Luke 23:34

Then Jesus said, "Father, forgive them, for they do not know what they do." And they divided His garments and cast lots.


## SOLDIERS GAMBLED FOR HIS COAT

**Prophecy**    Psalm 22:17, 18

I can count all My bones. They look *and* stare at Me.

   They divide My garments among them, and for My clothing they cast lots.

**Fulfilled**    Matthew 27:35, 36

Then they crucified Him, and divided His garments, casting lots, that it might be fulfilled which was spoken by the prophet: *"They divided My garments among them, and for My clothing they cast lots."*

Sitting down, they kept watch over Him there.

## NO BONES BROKEN

**Prophecy**  Psalm 34:20
He guards all his bones; not one of them is broken

**Fulfilled**  John 19:32, 33, 36
Then the soldiers came and broke the legs of the first and of the other who was crucified with Him.

But when they came to Jesus and saw that He was already dead, they did not break His legs.

For these things were done that the Scripture should be fulfilled, *"Not one of His bones shall be broken."*

## HIS SIDE PIERCED

**Prophecy**  Zechariah 12:10
"And I will pour on the house of David and on the inhabitants of Jerusalem the Spirit of grace and supplication; then they will look on Me whom they have pierced; they will mourn for Him as one mourns for *his* only *son,* and grieve for Him as one grieves for a firstborn."

**Fulfilled**  John 19:34
But one of the soldiers pierced His side with a spear, and immediately blood and water came out.

## BURIED WITH THE RICH

**Prophecy**  Isaiah 53:9
And they made His grave with the wicked—but with the rich at His death, because He had done no violence, nor *was any* deceit in His mouth.

**Fulfilled**    Matthew 27:57–60

Now when evening had come, there came a rich man from Arimathea, named Joseph, who himself had also become a disciple of Jesus.

This man went to Pilate and asked for the body of Jesus. Then Pilate commanded the body to be given to him.

And when Joseph had taken the body, he wrapped it in a clean linen cloth, and laid it in his new tomb which he had hewn out of the rock; and he rolled a large stone against the door of the tomb, and departed.


## TO BE RESURRECTED

**Prophecy**    Psalm 16:10

For You will not leave my soul in Sheol, nor will You allow Your Holy One to see corruption.

Psalm 49:15

But God will redeem my soul from the power of the grave, for He shall receive me. Selah

**Fulfilled**    Mark 16:6, 7

But he said to them, ''Do not be alarmed. You seek Jesus of Nazareth, who was crucified. He is risen! He is not here. See the place where they laid Him.

''But go *and* tell His disciples—and Peter—that He is going before you into Galilee; there you will see Him, as He said to you.''


## HIS ASCENSION TO GOD'S RIGHT HAND

**Prophecy**    Psalm 68:18

You have ascended on high, You have led captivity captive; You have received gifts among men, even *among* the rebellious, that the LORD God might dwell *there*.

**Fulfilled**    Mark 16:19

So then, after the Lord had spoken to them, He was received up into heaven, and sat down at the right hand of God.

1 Corinthians 15:4

And that He was buried, and that He rose again the third day according to the Scriptures.

Ephesians 4:8

Therefore He says: *"When He ascended on high, He led captivity captive, and gave gifts to men."*

# Where in the World?

1. **Eden was watered by what?**
   **A.** rain
   **B.** a river
   **C.** Adam and Eve
   **D.** angels

ANSWERS
p. 220

2. **Where did the ark rest after the flood?**
   **A.** Mt. Ararat
   **B.** Mt. Olives
   **C.** Mt. Horeb
   **D.** Mt. Rushmore

---

# HOW ABOUT THAT!

Psalm 117 is the exact middle of the Bible and also the shortest chapter in the Bible, with only two verses!

---

3. **What name did Jacob give the place where he dreamed about a ladder reaching to heaven?**
   **A.** Luz
   **B.** Bethel

---

**C.** Bed
**D.** Gerar

4. **Moses fled to which city after he killed the Egyptian?**
   **A.** Canaan
   **B.** Edom
   **C.** Midian
   **D.** Carson City

## MATCHING

| Place | Event |
|-------|-------|
| 1. Ur | a. Job's homeland |
| 2. Sodom and Gomorrah | b. 10 Commandments given |
| 3. Jericho | c. Alice falls in hole |
| 4. Moab | d. Abram's early life |
| 5. Uz | e. Rahab lives and helps spies |
| 6. Shushan | f. Saul's disobedient sacrifice |
| 7. Wonderland | g. Tower of Babel |
| 8. Gilgal | h. Esther becomes Queen |
| 9. Mt. Sinai | i. Moses died |
| 10. Shinar | j. God destroyed them |

# PUT THE FOLLOWING IN ORDER
## (where they lived, from birth to death)

**Abraham:**

1. Ur
2. Mamre
3. Mt. Moriah
4. Shechem
5. Haran
6. Bethel

ANSWERS
p. 221

**Jacob:**

1. Bethel
2. Penuel

3. Haran
4. Mamre
5. Beersheba
6. Egypt

## UNSCRAMBLE

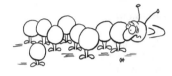

1. Deen
2. Oirjech
3. Doosm
4. Ru

5. Resial

6. Ybonlab

7. Zaratneh

8. More

9. Wen Kory Tyci

10. Nitorch

ANSWERS p. 222

## FILL IN THE BLANKS

1. Joseph took his family to _____ so that Herod could not kill Jesus.

2. _____ was the king of Judah when Jesus was born in Bethlehem.

3. "You, _____, who are exalted to heaven, will be brought down to Hades," was _____'s prediction about the city.

4. Jesus told Peter that He would give him the keys to _____.

5. Jesus arranged to meet his disciples at _____ after his resurrection.

# WORD BANK

| Heaven | Judea | Capernaum |
|--------|-------|-----------|
| Herod | Galilee | Egypt |

**TALL TALE**

When the disciples were _____
<sub>VERB (-ING)</sub>

through the city of _____, they
<sub>CITY</sub>

came upon a _____ who
<sub>NOUN</sub>

claimed to have met a famous rabbi. They asked him,

"_____," to which he replied that he
<sub>QUESTION</sub>

did not know. They _____ him,
<sub>VERB (PAST TENSE)</sub>

"Then how do you know you met him?" Because he was

_____ the _____ and talking
<sub>VERB (-ING)</sub> <sub>NOUNS</sub>

to the little children. The _____ dis-
<sub>ADJECTIVE</sub>

ciples were confused by this explanation. How could this

_____ think that _____
<sub>NOUN</sub> <sub>PRONOUN</sub>

_____ who this rabbi is? Have
<sub>VERB</sub>

# Top Ten Commandments Not Given on Mt. Sinai

**10.** Humor thy father and mother.

**9.** Thou shalt not mumble.

**8.** Thou shalt not remove thy mattress tags.

**7.** Remember thy Swiss cheese and keep it holy.

**6.** Remember thy shower and use it daily.

**5.** Thou shalt not toilet paper thy neighbor's house.

**4.** Thou shalt take thy IV in vein.

**3.** Try not to steal.

**2.** Thou shalt not covet thy neighbor's riding lawn-mower.

**1.** Remember the Alamo.

they seen him in the _____?
PRINT MATERIAL

Surely not. After they _____ and
VERB

_____, they came to the conclu-
VERB

sion that the _____ was right be-
NOUN

cause, _____!
EXCUSE

## TRUE OR FALSE

1. Jesus came from Nazareth to the Jordan to be baptized by John the Baptist.

2. Jesus was tempted on the Mount of Olives.

3. Simon and James were from Bethsaida.

4. John the Baptist's family lived in the hill country of Judah.

5. Nazareth was known as "The city of David."

---

Q. Which area of Palestine was particularly wealthy?

A. The area around the Jordan because the banks were always overflowing.

---

**6.** Capernaum was the home base of Jesus' travels during his ministry.

**7.** Jesus cleansed the temple during Passover in Bethlehem.

**8.** Jesus was in Galilee, near the sea, when the Jews took up stones to kill him for blasphemy.

**9.** The Jews led Jesus from Caiaphas to the Praetorium, but would not go inside so that they would not be defiled.

**10.** The apostles were in Jerusalem when Jesus told them to wait for the Promise of the Father.

**MULTIPLE CHOICE**

**1. Before his ascension, Jesus told the disciples to be witnesses to:**

**A.** Jerusalem

**B.** Judea and Samaria

**C.** the ends of the earth

**D.** all of the above

ANSWERS
p. 223

**2. Where did the disciples gather to wait for the gift of the Holy Spirit?**

**A.** the temple

**B.** an upper room

**C.** Mt. Olivet

**D.** Godot

3. **What is the name of the porch on the temple?**
   **A.** the outer court
   **B.** Solomon's porch
   **C.** the son room
   **D.** David's porch

4. **The road from Jerusalem to Gaza travels through which kind of terrain?**
   **A.** desert
   **B.** countryside
   **C.** mountains
   **D.** virtual reality

**MATCHING**

| Place | Event |
|-------|-------|
| **1.** Damascus | a. Disciples first called Christians |
| **2.** Corinth | b. Name means "little fountains" |
| **3.** Antioch | c. Phoebe delivers Paul's letter to this church |
| **4.** Galatia | d. Believer's turn to a different gospel |
| **5.** Ephesus | e. Converts include pagan idolaters, God-fearing Greeks, and Jews |

| Place | Event |
|-------|-------|
| 6. Philippi | f. Paul preaches first sermon |
| 7. Thessalonica | g. Philemon's hometown |
| 8. Colosse | h. Center for pagan worship and magical arts |
| 9. Rome | i. John writes Revelation here |
| 10. Patmos | j. Chloe's church is here |

## PUT THE FOLLOWING IN ORDER

**(Paul's first missionary journey from start to finish)**

1. Antioch
2. Pisidian Antioch
3. Derbe
4. Seleucia
5. Paphos
6. Perga
7. Attalia
8. Iconium
9. Lystra
10. Salamis

ANSWERS
p. 224

**(some will be used twice)**

1. **Which of the following were churches addressed in Revelation?**
   A. Pergamos
   B. Thyatira
   C. Sardis
   D. First Presbyterian
   E. Philadelphia
   F. All of the above

2. **In the throne room of Heaven there are which of the following:**
   A. a rainbow
   B. an emerald throne
   C. twenty-four thrones
   D. lightning and thunder
   E. lamps of fire
   F. a sea of glass, like crystal
   G. a McDonalds

3. **Where were the four angels standing when they opened the scrolls?**
   A. the throne room
   B. the four corners of the earth
   C. on their heads
   D. in the four churches

**4. Where does the River of Life proceed from?**
   **A.** the new Euphrates
   **B.** the tree of life
   **C.** God's throne
   **D.** the Lamb of God

ANSWERS
p. 225

# ANSWERS TO:
# WHERE IN THE WORLD?

## MULTIPLE CHOICE

| # ANSWER | REFERENCE |
|----------|-----------|
| 1. b | Genesis 2:10 |
| 2. a | Genesis 8:4 |
| 3. b | Genesis 28:19 |
| 4. c | Exodus 2:15 |

## MATCHING

| # ANSWER | REFERENCE |
|----------|-----------|
| 1. d | Genesis 11 |
| 2. j | Genesis 19 |
| 3. e | Joshua 2 |
| 4. i | Deuteronomy 34:5 |
| 5. a | Job 1 |
| 6. h | Esther 1:1 |
| 7. c | *Alice's Adventures in Wonderland* |
| 8. f | Joshua 4–6 |
| 9. b | Exodus 19 |
| 10. g | Genesis 11 |

# PUT THE FOLLOWING IN ORDER

| # ANSWER | REFERENCE |
|---|---|
| **Abraham:** | |
| 1. Ur; birthplace | Genesis 11:31 |
| 2. Haran; dwells with father, nephew Lot, and wife Sarai | Genesis 11:31–32 |
| 3. Shechem; builds altar at tere-binth tree of Moreh | Genesis 12:6,7 |
| 4. Bethel; builds altar at the mountain east of Bethel | Genesis 12:8 |
| 5. Mt. Moriah; Abraham takes Isaac to be sacrificed | Genesis 22 |
| 6. Mamre; buried | Genesis 25 |
| **Jacob:** | |
| 1. Beersheba; birthright | Genesis 27 |
| 2. Bethel; dreams of angels going up and down staircase to heaven | Genesis 28:1–19 |
| 3. Haran; marries Leah and Rachel | Genesis 29:14–28 |
| 4. Penuel; wrestles with an angel | Genesis 32:22–32 |
| 5. Egypt; travels to escape famine with 12 sons | Genesis 46:1–6 |
| 6. Mamre; buried | Genesis 50:13–14 |

## UNSCRAMBLE

| # ANSWER |
| --- |
| 1. Eden |
| 2. Jericho |
| 3. Sodom |
| 4. Ur |
| 5. Israel |
| 6. Babylon |
| 7. Nazareth |
| 8. Rome |
| 9. New York City |
| 10. Corinth |

## FILL IN THE BLANKS

| # ANSWER | REFERENCE |
| --- | --- |
| 1. Egypt | Matthew 2:14 |
| 2. Herod | Matthew 2:1 |
| 3. Capernaum, Jesus | Matthew 11:23 |
| 4. Heaven | Matthew 16:18–19 |
| 5. Galilee | Matthew 28:10 |

## TRUE OR FALSE

| # ANSWER | REFERENCE |
|---|---|
| 1. True | Mark 1:9 |
| 2. False; in the desert | Mark 1:12–13 |
| 3. False; Andrew and Peter | John 1:44 |
| 4. True | Luke 1:39–66 |
| 5. False; Bethlehem | Luke 2:4 |
| 6. True | Luke 4:31 |
| 7. False; Jerusalem | John 2:13–16 |
| 8. False; Jerusalem, in the temple | John 10:23, 31 |
| 9. True | John 18:28 |
| 10. True | Acts 1:4 |

## MULTIPLE CHOICE

| # ANSWER | REFERENCE |
|---|---|
| 1. d | Acts 1:8 |
| 2. b | Acts 1:13 |
| 3. b | Acts 3:11 |
| 4. a | Acts 8:26 |

## MATCHING

| # | ANSWER | REFERENCE |
|------|--------|-----------|
| 1. | f | Acts 9:19–20 |
| 2. | j | 1 Corinthians 1:11 |
| 3. | a | Acts 11:26 |
| 4. | d | Galatians 1:6 |
| 5. | h | Acts 19:35 |
| 6. | b | from the Greek, Krenides |
| 7. | e | 1 Thessalonians 1:8, 10 |
| 8. | g | Colossians 4:7–9 |
| 9. | c | Romans 16:1 |
| 10. | i | Revelation 1:9 |

## PUT THE FOLLOWING IN ORDER

| # | ANSWER | REFERENCE |
|------|--------|-----------|
| 1. | Antioch (In Syria) | Acts 13 |
| 2. | Seleucia (In Syria) | Acts 13 |
| 3. | Salamis (In Cyprus) | Acts 13 |
| 4. | Paphos (In Cyprus) | Acts 13 |
| 5. | Perga (Mediterranean Coast) | Acts 13 |
| 6. | Pisidian Antioch (In Phrygia) | Acts 13 |

| # ANSWER | REFERENCE |
|---|---|
| 7. Iconium (In Lycaonia) | Acts 14 |
| 8. Lystra (In Lycaonia) | Acts 14 |
| 9. Derbe (In Lycaonia) | Acts 14 |
| 10. Back to Lystra | |
| 11. Back to Iconium | |
| 12. Back to Pisidian Antioch | |
| 13. Back to Perga | |
| 14. To Attalia | |
| 15. Back to Seleucia | |
| 16. Back to Antioch | |

## MULTIPLE CHOICE

| # ANSWER | REFERENCE |
|---|---|
| 1. a,b,c,e | Revelation 2–3 |
| 2. a,b,c,d,e,f | Revelation 4 |
| 3. b | Revelation 7 |
| 4. c | Revelation 22 |

# Promises and Covenants

# TRUE OR FALSE

1. God's complete promise to Abraham was to make his descendents numerous and his nation great.

2. The Abrahamic covenant is the first promise in the Bible.

3. God promised to bless those who blessed Abraham.

4. God promised Noah that a flood will never again destroy the earth.

5. God made His covenant with Moses on Mt. Sinai.

6. In the Davidic covenant, God told David that He would be a Father to him.

7. God promised that David's kingdom and house would endure before Him forever.

8. Nathan delivered God's promise to David.

9. God made his covenant directly with "Abraham."

10. The Mosaic covenant was intended to replace the Abrahamic covenant.

# MULTIPLE CHOICE

1. **The Hebrew word for covenant is:**
   **A.** Qumran
   **B.** Mazel-Tov

---

**C.** Berit

**D.** Amen

2. **The three functions of the Mosaic covenant were to:**
   **A.** reveal God
   **B.** invent a perpetual motion machine
   **C.** reveal sin
   **D.** define God's expectations for man

---

# HOW ABOUT THAT!

The New Covenant is first mentioned in the book of Jeremiah (31:31), which has more words than any other book in the Bible.

---

3. **Which covenants are found in Genesis?**
   **A.** Davidic
   **B.** Adamic
   **C.** Abrahamic
   **D.** New

4. **In the Abrahamic covenant, God first commands Abraham to:**
   **A.** sacrifice his son, Isaac
   **B.** get out of his country and away from his family and father's house

**C.** build an altar

**D.** start a pyramid scheme

5. **Abraham thought he had fulfilled God's covenant when:**
   **A.** he built an altar
   **B.** he left his home
   **C.** he made a hole in one on the 13th while playing with Lot
   **D.** Ishmael was born

6. **What did God do when Abraham asked how he knew the covenant would come to pass:**
   **A.** passed a smoking oven and burning torch between a sacrifice
   **B.** commanded him to be silent
   **C.** gave him a 3-pound kidney stone
   **D.** fulfilled the covenant

ANSWERS p. 243

7. **When did God change Abraham's name from Abram?**
   **A.** when He first appeared to him
   **B.** after he left his home at age 75
   **C.** when he was 99 years old
   **D.** after Isaac was born

8. **Who laughed when God promised Abraham and Sarah a child?**
   **A.** Abraham
   **B.** Sarah
   **C.** Isaac
   **D.** their pet hyena

## FILL IN THE BLANKS

1. God saved Noah from the Flood because he was "_____ before God."

2. Noah and his family were in the ark for _____ days, but the rain only lasted _____ days.

3. God's promise to Noah was: "I will never again curse the _____ for _____'s sake, although the imagination of man's heart is _____

from his _____; nor will I
again destroy every living thing as I _____
_____."

4. God promises that seedtime and harvest, _____
and _____, _____ and
_____, and day and night would last as
long as the _____.

5. God blessed Noah and gave the _____ into
his hand.

6. God told Noah and his sons to _____
_____ and _____, and fill the earth.

7. The _____ is a sign of God's covenant with
Noah to never destroy the earth _____
_____ again.

8. God's covenant with Noah had _____
requirements for mankind.

---

Q. Why did God promise not to destroy the earth
by water again?
A. Because He knew his office would be flooded
with complaints!

---

## WORD BANK

| | | | |
|---|---|---|---|
| righteous | cold | cute | multiply |
| smile | by flood | have done | |
| man | 40 | heat | cloud |
| animals | evil | by lightning | |
| no | 150 | ground | |
| youth | summer | earth | |
| be fruitful | rainbow | | |
| munchkins | winter | | |

## MATCHING

**1.** Adam

a. eat dust all the days of your life

**2.** Eve

b. sorrow will multiply

**3.** Serpent

c. enmity between you and the woman

d. in toil you shall eat

e. in sweat you shall eat

f. your desire shall be for a mate

ANSWERS
p. 245

**3.** Serpent—cont'd    g. you will return to dust

h. your clothes will be made from animal skins

i. you will be sent out of the garden

## SHORT ANSWER

**1.** Who brought news of God's covenant with David to David? _____

**2.** When did the word of the Lord come to Nathan? _____

**3.** What had David desired to do before he learned of the covenant? _____

**4.** What did God tell David He would do for the people of Israel? _____

**5.** Why was David not to build a Temple? _____

**6.** What would be established forever? _____

**7.** God promised to do what to Solomon, as well as establish his throne? _____

**8.** What was David's response to God's covenant?

_____

_____

_____

## FILL IN THE BLANKS

**1.** God promises, in Amos 9, to _____ the damages to the tabernacle of David.''

**2.** God shows his mercy on his people in Hosea 2 when he says, ''I will _____ you to me in righteousness and justice, lovingkindness and mercy.''

**3.** In Isaiah 1 God says, ''If you are willing and _____, you shall eat the good of the land.''

**4.** God tells Israel in Jeremiah 3, ''I am _____ to you . . . I will bring you to Zion.''

**5.** The coming of the Messiah is foretold in Micah 5, ''But you, Bethlehem . . . out of you shall come forth to Me the One to be Ruler in _____.''

**6.** God severely punished Israel in Ezekiel 5 because they ''rebelled against my judgements by doing more _____ than all the countries around her."

7. In Joel 2, God promises that He is "slow to anger and of great kindness, and _____ from doing harm."

All of these are examples of a _____ of God.

## WORD BANK

| forget | repair | obedient |
| relents | Israel | betroth |
| wickedness | married | |

**MULTIPLE CHOICE**

1. **God promised Jacob that He would:**
   **A.** allow 7 sequels to Police Academy
   **B.** not leave until He fulfilled His Word
   **C.** make him the ruler of many people
   **D.** give him a place of honor among his people

2. **Joseph's promise of power over his brothers came to him in a(n):**

# Top Ten Beatitudes That Didn't Make It

**10.** Blessed are the poor in wallet, for they shall be called mooches.

**9.** Blessed are those who mourn, for they shall receive Prozac.

**8.** Blessed are the geeks, for they shall make billions developing computer software.

**7.** Blessed are those who hunger and thirst, for they shall give McDonalds their business.

**6.** Blessed are those with rich relatives, for they shall inherit a fortune.

**5.** Blessed are the landscapers, for they shall see sod.

**4.** Blessed are the pure in heart, for they shall not need angioplasty.

**3.** Blessed are the pacemakers.

**2.** Blessed are those with Chex Mix, for they shall be the life of the party.

**1.** Blessed are you when people say all manner of evil against you falsely, for you shall be able to sue for slander.

**A.** dream about gold

**B.** instant message

**C.** dream about wheat

**D.** vision of famine

3. **God promised Moses what, which was the opposite of his fears:**

    **A.** power

    **B.** wealth

    **C.** that his toses weren't roses

    **D.** success

ANSWERS
p. 246

4. **God promised to give Solomon which of his requests:**

    **A.** wisdom

    **B.** riches

    **C.** honor

    **D.** popularity with the ladies

5. **Naaman believed the prophet's promise of healing from what disease:**

    **A.** blindness

    **B.** strep throat

    **C.** lame feet

    **D.** leprosy

6. **Because Jehu did what was right in God's sight, God promised him:**

    **A.** that his sons would sit on the throne for four generations

    **B.** that he would rule a nation

**C.** a great stock option plan

**D.** wealth and prosperity

7. **Isaiah assured Hezekiah that his enemy would turn and go to his own land because:**

    **A.** he will be afraid of the size of Hezekiah's army

    **B.** his land will be attacked

    **C.** he will hear a rumor about his home

    **D.** he will get homesick for his momma

8. **God promised Josiah that he would not see**

    **A.** the death of his sons

    **B.** the calamity He would bring on this place

    **C.** the end of the reign of David

    **D.** any of the sequels to Police Academy

## FILL IN THE BLANKS

1. The angel promised Mary she would _____ in her womb and bring forth a _____.

2. He also told her that Jesus would reign over the house of _____ forever.

3. After Peter declared Jesus was the Christ, Jesus said to him, "Blessed are you Simon _____, . . . on this _____ I will build my church."

**4.** Jesus promised the _____ that "there are some standing here who will not taste _____ until they see the kingdom of God _____ with power."

**5.** Jesus promised the disciples that they would receive the _____ _____ when He departed from them.

**6.** Jesus promised the thief on the cross that _____ they would meet in _____.

**7.** Zacharias was struck _____ when he questioned the promise of a _____.

**8.** The church elders (in 1 Peter 5) are promised a
_____ of _____ that does not _____.

## WORD BANK

Bar-Jonah     fade     today

Son     crown     conceive

Paradise     Jacob     present

death     son     Holy Spirit

disciples     rock     glory     mute

# ANSWERS TO:
# PROMISES AND COVENANTS

## TRUE OR FALSE

| # ANSWER | REFERENCE |
|---|---|
| 1. False; and make his name great. | Genesis 12:2–7 |
| 2. False; the first promise is that the Seed of the woman shall bruise the head of the serpent. | Genesis 3:14ff |
| 3. True | Genesis 12:2 |
| 4. True | Genesis 9 |
| 5. True | Exodus 19–20 |
| 6. False; God would be a father to David's seed. | 2 Samuel 7 |
| 7. True | 2 Samuel 7 |
| 8. True | 2 Samuel 7 |
| 9. False; with "Abram." | Genesis 12 |
| 10. False; the Law does not replace God's promise to Abraham. | Galatians 3:15–18 |

## MULTIPLE CHOICE

| # ANSWER | REFERENCE |
|---|---|
| 1. c | |
| 2. a,c,d | |

| # ANSWER | REFERENCE |
|----------|-----------|
| 3. b,c | Genesis 3, 15 |
| 4. b | Genesis 12 |
| 5. d | Genesis 15 |
| 6. a | Genesis 15 |
| 7. c | Genesis 17 |
| 8. b | |

## FILL IN THE BLANKS

| # ANSWER | REFERENCE |
|----------|-----------|
| 1. righteous | Genesis 7 |
| 2. 365, 40 | Genesis 7–8 |
| 3. ground, man's, evil, youth, have done | Genesis 8 |
| 4. cold, heat, winter, summer, earth | Genesis 8 |
| 5. animals | Genesis 9 |
| 6. be fruitful, multiply | Genesis 9 |
| 7. rainbow, by flood | Genesis 9 |
| 8. no | Genesis 9 |

# MATCHING

| # ANSWER | REFERENCE |
|---|---|
| 1. d,e,g,h,i | Genesis 2 |
| 2. b,f,h,i | |
| 3. a,c | |

# SHORT ANSWER

| # ANSWER |
|---|
| 1. Nathan |
| 2. at night |
| 3. build a Temple |
| 4. appoint a place for them |
| 5. God didn't desire one at the time—Solomon should build it. |
| 6. David's house and throne |
| 7. discipline him |
| 8. He praised Him and dedicated Israel to Him. |

# FILL IN THE BLANKS

| # ANSWER |
|---|
| 1. repair |
| 2. betroth |

## FILL IN THE BLANKS—cont'd

| # | ANSWER |
|---|--------|
| 3. | obedient |
| 4. | married |
| 5. | Israel |
| 6. | wickedness |
| 7. | relents |

## MULTIPLE CHOICE

| # | ANSWER | REFERENCE |
|---|--------|-----------|
| 1. | b | Genesis 28:15 |
| 2. | c | Genesis 37:5 |
| 3. | d | Exodus 3:18 |
| 4. | a | 1 Kings 3 |
| 5. | d | 2 Kings 5 |
| 6. | a | 2 Kings 10 |
| 7. | c | Isaiah 37 |
| 8. | b | 2 Kings 22 |

## FILL IN THE BLANKS

| # ANSWER | REFERENCE |
|----------|-----------|
| 1. conceive, Son | Luke 1 |
| 2. Jacob | Luke 1 |
| 3. Bar-Jonah, rock | Matt 16 |
| 4. disciples, death, present | Mark 9 |
| 5. Holy Spirit | Acts 1:8 |
| 6. today, Paradise | Luke 23:43 |
| 7. mute, son | Luke 1:13 |
| 8. crown, glory, fade | 1 Peter 5 |

# PROMISES IN SCRIPTURE

## WHAT TO DO WHEN YOU ARE . . .

**Afraid**
2 Timothy 1:7
Romans 8:15–16
1 John 4:18
Psalm 91:4–7
Hebrews 13:6, 8
John 14:27

**Angry**
Proverbs 14:16, 17, 29
Proverbs 16:32
Ecclesiastes 7:9
Romans 12:19
Ephesians 4:26
James 1:19–20

**Anxious**
Proverbs 3:24
Psalm 92:1–2
Matthew 6:25–44
John 14:27
Hebrews 4:3, 9
Psalm 4:8

**Confused**
Proverbs 3:5–6
Psalm 32:8
2 Timothy 1:7

## What to Do When You Are . . . Confused

Isaiah 43:2
Philippians 4:6, 7
James 1:5

### Depressed

Isaiah 43:2
Psalm 30:5
Isaiah 61:3
2 Corinthians 1:3, 4
Philippians 4:8
Nehemiah 8:10

### Despairing

Ezekiel 34:16
Psalm 100:5
Jeremiah 32:17
Isaiah 40:29
Ephesians 1:18
Psalm 119:116

### Disappointed

James 4:2–3
John 15:7
Psalm 10:17
Mark 11:24
Psalm 33:18
Ephesians 3:20

### Discouraged

Isaiah 51:11
Hebrews 10:35, 36

## What to Do When You Are . . . Discouraged

Galatians 6:9
Psalm 27:1–14
Psalm 42:11
Isaiah 40:30–31

### Dissatisfied

Psalm 37:3
Psalm 63:1–5
Proverbs 12:14
Psalm 103:1–5
Isaiah 12:2–3
Matthew 5:6

### Disobedient

Luke 11:28
John 15:10
1 John 2:5
Psalm 119:35
John 8:31–32
John 14:23

### Doubtful

Romans 10:17
Isaiah 55:10, 11
Mark 11:22–24
Luke 12:29–31
2 Peter 3:9
Psalm 18:30

### Forsaken

1 Samuel 16:7
1 Chronicles 28:9

## What to Do When You Are . . . Forsaken

Psalm 1:1–3
Romans 8:37
Psalm 37:5–7
Colossians 3:12–14

### Frustrated
Philippians 2:4
James 1:12
1 Peter 4:8
Ephesians 4:31–32
Psalm 37:8–9
Psalm 141:3

### Grieving
Matthew 5:4
2 Thessalonians 2:16–17
1 Corinthians 15:55–57
Revelation 21:4
Hebrew 4:15
Psalm 23:4
John 14:3

### Guilty
1 Corinthians 6:11
Nehemiah 9:17
Psalm 130:4–5
Jeremiah 33:8
John 3:18
Isaiah 43:25

### Impatient
Isaiah 40:31
Lamentations 3:26

## What to Do When You Are . . . Impatient

Hebrews 10:35–37
Romans 15:4–5
Psalm 40:1
Hebrews 12:1

## Insecure

Hebrews 13:18
Ephesians 1:18–19
Philippians 1:9–11
Colossians 3:16
John 17:11
Ephesians 3:18–19

## Lonely

Matthew 28:20
Isaiah 41:10
Deuteronomy 31:6
Romans 8:35–36
Deuteronomy 33:27

## Longing

Psalm 145:19
Psalm 119:37
Proverbs 16:3
Philippians 4:12–13
Proverbs 16:9
Psalm 84:11

## Persecuted

Matthew 5:10
2 Samuel 22:4

## What to Do When You Are . . . Persecuted

Psalm 103:6
Jeremiah 20:13
1 Peter 3:11–12
Psalm 32:10

### Rebellious

1 Samuel 15:22–23
Philippians 2:5–8
1 Peter 5:5–6
Romans 6:12–13
Ephesians 5:8

### Suffering

Romans 5:3–4
1 Peter 3:14
Psalm 34:19
1 Peter 2:20–21
Isaiah 42:16
Job 2:10

### Tempted

Psalm 119:11
Proverbs 28:13
Hebrews 4:14–16
1 Peter 5:8–9
2 Peter 2:9
1 Corinthians 10:12–13

### Weak

Psalm 142:3
Psalm 147:6

## What to Do When You Are . . . Weak

Habakkuk 3:19
1 Chronicles 16:11
Isaiah 57:15
2 Corinthians 12:9

# When the Saints Go Marching In

## MULTIPLE CHOICE

1. **St. Ambrose of Milan was elected bishop when:**
   **A.** he healed a woman of her lifelong disease
   **B.** he won the majority of the electoral college
   **C.** a little boy cried out, "Ambrose, bishop!"
   **D.** he received a revelation from God

2. **St. Ambrose dedicated himself to the eradication of:**
   **A.** Arianism
   **B.** Gnosticism
   **C.** Materialism
   **D.** Marcionism

ANSWERS
p. 272

3. **On which major holiday was Ambrose buried?**
   **A.** Christmas
   **B.** Easter
   **C.** Palm Sunday
   **D.** Flag Day

4. **St. Augustine of Canterbury was called:**
   **A.** Bob
   **B.** Servant to the Anglo-Saxon
   **C.** Apostle to the English
   **D.** Disciple to the British

5. **Why was Augustine sent to England?**
   **A.** They had received no missionaries.
   **B.** He wanted to see the Tower of London.

**C.** He spoke Anglo-Saxon.

**D.** Pope St. Gregory the Great believed the English were as beautiful as angels.

6. **Which Augustine wrote *The Confessions of St. Augustine*?**
   **A.** St. Augustine of Canterbury
   **B.** St. Augustine of Hippo
   **C.** St. Augustine of St. Louis
   **D.** St. Augustine of Rome

7. **St. Augustine of Hippo was born in which country?**
   **A.** Numidia (modern-day Algeria)
   **B.** The United States of America
   **C.** Italy (Rome)
   **D.** Crete

8. **Basil the Great had two siblings who also became:**
   **A.** spices
   **B.** missionaries
   **C.** saints
   **D.** "the Great"s

---

Q. How did St. Boniface get a black eye?
A. He called St. Francis a sissy.

---

## MATCHING

1. Basil the Great

2. Bernard de Clairvaux

3. Clement of Alexandria

4. Venerable Bede

5. Thomas Cranmer

6. John Donne

7. Bonaventure

8. Cornelius the Centurion

9. Francis of Assisi

10. Gregory the Illuminator

a. *Ecclesiastical History of the English People*

b. Franciscan monk healed by St. Francis

c. 2nd century bishop of Caesarea

d. patron saint of animals

e. Father of Eastern Monasticism

f. attended Oxford University at age twelve

g. brought Christianity to Armenia

h. founded Alexandrian School of Theology

i. *Book of Common Prayer*

j. sponsored the formation of the Knights Templars—warrior monks who fought in the first Crusade

## FILL IN THE BLANKS

1. Bonaventure was born in _____ and followed the teachings of St. _____.

**2.** Brigid of Kildare founded the first _____

_____ _____ in Ireland.

**3.** Clare of Assisi followed St. _____ and began

a group of nuns called the _____.

**4.** _____ _____, while being burned at

the stake, said, "As my _____ offended in

writing contrary to my heart, my _____ shall

first be punished," and stuck his _____ in

the fire.

**5.** St. Etheldreda had a large swelling on her _____

that she believed was punishment for her earlier love

of lavish _____.

**6.** St. Francis of Assisi was _____-_____

years old when he realized his calling in life.

**7.** St. _____ had a famous fire.

**8.** Ignatius of Loyola served as a boy page in the Span-

ish court of _____ and _____.

## WORD BANK

neck     Ferdinand     Paul

Francis     thirty-one     Italy

Isabella     necklaces     Elmo

Minoresses     maidens     hand

twenty-two     Egypt

Elizabeth     Thomas Cranmer

women's religious order

**PUT THE
FOLLOWING
IN ORDER
(from earliest to latest in history)**

1. Venerable Bede
2. Bonaventure
3. St. Francis of Assisi
4. Hugh Latimer
5. Ignatius of Loyola
6. Irenaeus of Lyons
7. Jerome
8. Julian of Norwich
9. Justin Martyr
10. Monnica

ANSWERS
p. 274

## SHORT ANSWER

1. St. Ignatius of Loyola founded what religious society? _____

2. Irenaeus of Lyon's name appropriately means what? _____

3. What is St. Jerome's most remembered accomplishment? _____ _____

4. John of the Cross and Teresa of Avila were cofounders of what? _____

5. Dame Julian of Norwich was one of what group of Christians? _____

6. When did the Saints last win a Super Bowl? _____

7. How did Justin Martyr die? _____

8. Who cried out, while being burned at the stake, ". . . by God's grace we shall this day light such a candle in England as I trust shall never be put out!"? _____

## UNSCRAMBLE

1. Mothas Quniaas
2. Celsausnew
3. Matsoh à Kebtec
4. Hosamt à Peksim
5. Restea fo Viaal
6. Katpicr fo Lernida
7. Teprepau
8. Lyopracp fo Mysnar
9. Sotham Remo
10. Ryneh Ymratn

ANSWERS p. 275

# HOW ABOUT THAT!

In order to be a saint, a person must be able to be in direct contact with God—Pure Awareness.

## MULTIPLE CHOICE

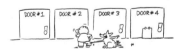

1. **St. Lucy of Sicily is symbolized by a lamp representing her pledge of:**

A. allegiance
B. virginity
C. silence
D. a chicken in the pot of every peasant

2. Lucy's name means "light," so she was considered:
   A. a protector of the blind
   B. underweight
   C. a beacon
   D. a judge

3. St. Lucy's other symbol, which no one can explain the significance of, is:
   A. a mouse
   B. an ostrich
   C. a blind camel
   D. a cat

4. St. Margaret of Scotland brought whose reforms to the church of Scotland:
   A. John of the Cross
   B. John Wycliff
   C. Saint Gregory VII
   D. Wyclef Jean

5. Henry Martyn served as a chaplain for:
   A. the Notre Dame football team
   B. House of Commons
   C. The East India Company
   D. The Royal Palace

**6. Monnica was the mother of:**
   **A.** Pearl
   **B.** St. Augustine of Hippo
   **C.** St. Augustine of Canterbury
   **D.** St. Francis of Assisi

ANSWERS
p. 276

**7. Monnica's name in Greek means:**
   **A.** One Victory
   **B.** Peace with God
   **C.** half of a harmonica
   **D.** one day

**8. Thomas More is a saint in which communion:**
   **A.** North Pole
   **B.** Protestant

**C.** Catholic
**D.** Anglican

**TRUE OR FALSE**

1. St. Margaret of Scotland never married.

2. St. Patrick traveled to Ireland from Rome.

3. St. Patrick was kidnapped and sold into slavery in Ireland.

4. St. Patrick used a shamrock, the three-leaved cousin to a clover, to teach the principles of the Trinity.

5. Perpetua was condemned to death at the arena and was killed by wild animals.

6. When Perpetua's executioner failed to kill her, she guided his sword toward her own death.

7. Nicholas Ridley wrote the *Book of Common Prayer.*

8. Scholastica is considered the mother of women's monasticism in the Western Church.

9. The Saint, Val Kilmer, was a man of many names.

10. Elizabeth Ann Seton was the first native-born American to be canonized as a saint.

# Top Ten People Groups Still in Need of a Patron Saint

10. Parents of children with science projects due

9. The gingivitis inflicted

8. The sleep deprived

7. Internet junkies

6. Heartburn sufferers

5. The balding

4. Third-string NFL quarterbacks

3. The toothless

2. Fourth-year, undeclared-major college students

1. Chronically late employees

## MATCHING

1. Swithun of Winchester

2. Thomas Aquinas

3. Theresa of Lisieux

4. Wenceslaus

5. Thomas à Becket

6. Elizabeth Ann Seton

7. William Tyndale

8. Alban

9. Teresa of Avila

10. Thomas à Kempis

a. canonized for work with poor and orphans

b. if it rains on his feast day, then it will rain 40 more days

c. ran away from home at age 7 to become a martyr

d. last words were verified: "After my death, I will let fall a shower of roses."

e. Bible translator burned at the stake

f. patron saint of Bohemia

g. murdered in the Canterbury Cathedral

h. wrote *Imitation of Christ*

i. first British martyr

j. brilliant scholar who was called "Dumb Ox" by classmates

1. What was Alcuin's greatest contribution to his society? _____

_____

2. What did Ambrose do to end paganism in the Roman Empire? _____

3. What did St. Antony of Egypt never see for twenty years? _____

**4.** What saint was St. Benedict of Nursia's twin sister?

_____

**5.** St. Blaise is the patron saint of what? _____

_____

**6.** St. Boniface of Mainz convinced the people of the Netherlands of the power of God by doing what?

_____

_____

**7.** St. Catherine of Siena, the youngest of twenty-five children, worked as what? _____

**8.** St. Cyril and St. Methodius were missionaries to what people? _____

## FILL IN THE BLANKS

**1.** Edward the _____ is called this because he dedicated himself to the faith, faced _____, but was not _____.

**2.** Fabian of Rome was elected _____ when a _____ landed on his head.

**3.** St. _____ is the patron saint of England.

**4.** _____ is revered by the _____
Church and is considered the patron saint of Russia.

### WORD BANK

ANSWERS
p. 278

| | | |
|---|---|---|
| frightened | George | dove |
| martyred | Eastern | Sergius |
| the mob | confessor | Pope |
| tailor | governor | saint | death |

# ANSWERS TO:
# WHEN THE SAINTS GO MARCHING IN

## MULTIPLE CHOICE

| # | ANSWER |
|---|--------|
| 1. | c |
| 2. | a |
| 3. | b |
| 4. | c |
| 5. | d |
| 6. | b |
| 7. | a |
| 8. | c |

## MATCHING

| # | ANSWER |
|---|--------|
| 1. | e |
| 2. | j |
| 3. | h |
| 4. | a |

## # ANSWER

5. i

6. f

7. b

8. c

9. d

10. g

## FILL IN THE BLANKS

### # ANSWER

1. Italy, Francis

2. women's religious order

3. Francis, Minoresses

4. Thomas Cranmer, hand, hand, hand

5. neck, necklaces

6. twenty-two

7. Elmo

8. Ferdinand, Isabella

## PUT THE FOLLOWING IN ORDER

| # ANSWER | DATE |
|----------|------|
| 9. Justin Martyr | A.D. 110 |
| 6. Irenaeus of Lyons | A.D. 125 |
| 10. Monnica | A.D. 331 |
| 7. Jerome | A.D. 340 |
| 1. Venerable Bede | A.D. 673 |
| 3. Francis of Assisi | A.D. 1182 |
| 2. Bonaventure | A.D. 1221 |
| 8. Julian of Norwich | A.D. 1342 |
| 4. Hugh Latimer | A.D. 1490 |
| 5. Ignatius of Loyola | A.D. 1491 |

## SHORT ANSWER

**# ANSWER**

1. Jesuits

2. Peaceful One

3. the Vulgate Bible—translated entire Bible into Latin from Hebrew and Greek

| # | ANSWER |
|---|--------|
| 4. | the Order of Discalced Carmelites |
| 5. | mystics |
| 6. | never |
| 7. | in the arena, as a martyr |
| 8. | Hugh Latimer |

## UNSCRAMBLE

| # | ANSWER |
|---|--------|
| 1. | Thomas Aquinas |
| 2. | Wenceslaus |
| 3. | Thomas à Becket |
| 4. | Thomas à Kempis |
| 5. | Teresa of Avila |
| 6. | Patrick of Ireland |
| 7. | Perpetua |
| 8. | Polycarp of Smyrna |
| 9. | Thomas More |
| 10. | Henry Martyn |

## MULTIPLE CHOICE

| # | ANSWER |
|---|--------|
| 1. | b |
| 2. | a |
| 3. | d |
| 4. | c |
| 5. | c |
| 6. | b |
| 7. | a |
| 8. | d |

## TRUE OR FALSE

| # | ANSWER | REFERENCE |
|---|--------|-----------|
| 1. | False | married to a King |
| 2. | False | born and raised in Britain |
| 3. | True | |
| 4. | True | |
| 5. | False | only injured, not killed |

| # | ANSWER | REFERENCE |
|---|--------|-----------|
| 6. | True | |
| 7. | False | helped Thomas Cranmer write it |
| 8. | True | |
| 9. | True | |
| 10. | True | |

## MATCHING

| # | ANSWER |
|---|--------|
| 1. | b |
| 2. | j |
| 3. | d |
| 4. | f |
| 5. | g |
| 6. | a |
| 7. | e |
| 8. | i |
| 9. | c |
| 10. | h |

## SHORT ANSWER

| # | ANSWER |
|---|--------|
| 1. | the revival of quality education, first-rate schools and universities all over Europe |
| 2. | rallied cities against the Goths, who were destroyed |
| 3. | a human face |
| 4. | St. Scholastica |
| 5. | throat diseases, because he saved a boy from choking on a fishbone |
| 6. | chopping down a rotten tree—he was denouncing the pagan god Donar, whose symbol was the oak |
| 7. | a nurse to lepers and cancer victims |
| 8. | the Slavs |

## FILL IN THE BLANKS

| # | ANSWER |
|---|--------|
| 1. | Confessor, death, martyred |
| 2. | Pope, dove |
| 3. | George |
| 4. | Sergius, Eastern |

# THE INTERESTING AND UNUSUAL

## 1. HISTORY

It has been reported that the Bible has been the largest seller of all books published.

The Bible was written by about 40 men who engaged in writing it during a period of about 1600 years dating from 1500 B.C. to about 100 years after Christ. These men wrote as they were moved by the Holy Spirit (2 Pet. 1:21). They wrote not in words of human wisdom but in words taught by the Holy Ghost (1 Corinthians 2:13).

## 2. ENGLISH BIBLE

The first translation of the English Bible was initiated by John Wycliffe and completed by John Purvey in 1388.

The first American edition of the Bible was perhaps published some time before 1752.

The Bible has been translated in part or in whole (as of 1964) in over 1,200 different languages or dialects.

The Bible was divided into chapters by Stephen Langton about A.D. 1228.

The Old Testament was divided into verses by R. Nathan in A.D. 1448 and the New Testament by Robert Stephanus in A.D. 1551.

The entire Bible divided into chapters and verses first appeared in the Geneva Bible of 1560.

## 3. BOOKS OF THE BIBLE

Books of Bible ............................................. 66
The Old Testament ....................................... 39
The New Testament ....................................... 27

Middle book of Old Testament ................. Proverbs
Middle book of New Testament ......... 2 Thessalonians

## 4. CHAPTERS OF THE BIBLE

### A. Facts and figures
Entire Bible ............................. 1189 chapters
Old Testament ........................... 929 chapters
New Testament ....................... 260 chapters
Middle chapter of Old
    Testament ............................. Job 29
Middle chapter of New
    Testament ............................. Romans 13
Middle and shortest chapter
    of the Bible .......................... Psalm 117
Longest chapter in the Bible ......... Psalm 119
Chapters that are alike
    in the Bible .......................... 2 Kings 19;
                                            Isaiah 37

### B. Great Golden Chapters
Ascension ..................................... Acts 1
Backsliders.................................... Hosea 14
Beatitudes .................................... Matthew 5,6,7
Bread of Life .............................. John 6
Brotherhood ............................... Romans 14
Builders ..................................... Nehemiah 4
Burden-bearers .......................... Galatians 6
Call, Universal ........................... Isaiah 55
Call, Workers.............................. Isaiah 6
Chastening ................................. 2 Corinthians 4
Comfort....................................... Psalm 23:4
Confession .................................. Psalm 51
Consecration................................ Philemon 3
Constancy .................................. Ruth 1
Contrast ..................................... Deuteronomy
                                            28

## 5. VERSES

Shortest verse of the Old
   Testament ..............................1 Chronicles 1:25
Shortest verse of the New
   Testament ..............................John 11:35
Longest verse in the Bible ...........Esther 8:9
Verse containing all letters of
   the alphabet except J: ..............Ezra 7:21
Verse containing all letters of the
   alphabet except Q and M: ........Daniel 4:37
Verses alike: ............................Psalm 107:8, 15,
                                             21, 31

## 6. WORDS

In the Old Testament ................. c. 592,601 words
In the New Testament ................. c. 178,282 words

### Special Words in the Bible

Longest word in the Bible is:
   Maher-shalal-hash-baz
   (18 letters) .............................Isaiah 8:1

### Words Occurring Only Once in the Bible

Advocate ...................................1 John 2:1
Chair ........................................2 Kings 4:10
Fervor ......................................Zechariah 8:2
Gnat .........................................Matthew 23:24
''And'' occurs 38,800 times in the Bible.
Father, Father's, Fathers, Fathers' occur in the Bible
   1,645 times
Mother, Mothers, Mother's, Mothers' occur 321 times
Boy and boys occur 11 times
Girl and girls occur 26 times
God occurs 4,393 times
Lord occurs 7,766 times

## 7. LETTERS

In Old Testament .............................. c. 2,546,906
In New Testament .............................. c. 774,730

## 8. UNUSUAL THINGS IN THE BIBLE

1. Man who lived to be 969
   years old ........................Genesis 5:27
2. Sons of God married the
   daughters of men ...........Genesis 6:2
3. Man used a stone for a pil-
   low ...............................Genesis 28:11
4. Baby had a scarlet thread
   tied around its hand before
   it was born.....................Genesis 38:28–29
5. Battle won because man
   stretched out his hand ......Exodus 17:11
6. Man was spoken to by an
   ass ..............................Numbers 22:28–30
7. One who had a bed 13½
   feet long and 6 feet wide ...Deuteronomy 3:11
8. The women who had to
   shave their heads before
   they could marry ...........Deuteronomy 21:11–13
9. Women forbidden to wear
   men's clothing ..............Deuteronomy 22:5
10. Sun stood still for a whole
    day ............................Joshua 10:13
11. A woman killed a man by
    driving a nail through his
    head ..........................Judges 4:17–21
12. Men lapped water like
    dogs ...........................Judges 7:5
13. An army with seven hun-
    dred left-handed men ......Judges 20:16

14. Man whose hair weighed about 6⅔ lbs. when it was cut annually .................2 Samuel 14:26

15. Where a ferry boat was used..............................2 Samuel 19:18

16. Man who had twelve fingers and twelve toes........2 Samuel 21:20

17. The ax that floated in the water ...........................2 Kings 6:1–6

18. Woman boiled and ate her son .............................2 Kings 6:29

19. Man had seven hundred wives and three hundred concubines ...................1 Kings 11:3

20. Father who had eighty-eight children .................2 Chronicles 11:21

21. No taste in the white of an egg .............................Job 6:6

22. The sun travelled backward .....................Isaiah 38:8

23. Man walked naked for three years ....................Isaiah 20:2–3

24. Army of 185,000 destroyed in one night .................Isaiah 37:36

25. A man whose life was increased by 15 years because he prayed...............Isaiah 38:1–5

26. The Bible that was cut with a pen knife .....................Jeremiah 36:20–23

27. Graveyard full of dead bones resurrected ...........Ezekiel 37; 1–14

28. A harlot an ancestor of Christ ..........................Matthew 1:5

29. Man ate locusts for food ...Matthew 3:4

# Worship

## FILL IN THE BLANKS

1. The earliest musical activity of the Christian Church was _____ _____.

2. "Praise God from whom all _____ flow. Praise him all _____ here below. Praise him _____ ye heavenly hosts. Praise _____, _____, and Holy _____."

3. The Lesser Doxology is also known as the _____ _____.

4. The Greater Doxology is also known as the _____ _____ _____.

ANSWERS
p. 305

### WORD BANK

| | | |
|---|---|---|
| singing | blessings | creatures |
| Gloria | hymn | Son |
| | Ghost | Patri |
| Excelsis | Gloria in | Father |
| | above all | |

1. Dr. Babcock, who wrote the hymn, "This is my Father's World," saw nature as:
   A. the eagle's natural habitat
   B. the music of the spheres
   C. worthy of worship
   D. a mighty warrior

2. The hymn, "Beneath the Cross of Jesus" was written by which woman?
   A. Elizabeth Elliot
   B. Mother Teresa
   C. Elizabeth C. Clephane
   D. Fanny J. Crosby

3. John Bowring, the author of the hymn, "In the Cross of Christ I Glory," could speak how many languages before he died?
   A. 3
   B. 20
   C. over 100
   D. 33

4. The hymn "There is a Fountain" by William Cowper is based upon what Old Testament text?
   A. Zechariah 13:1
   B. Psalm 1:3
   C. Genesis 8:2
   D. Job 22:12

5. "There is a Fountain" was originally titled:
   **A.** Let the River Flow
   **B.** Peace for the Fountain Opened
   **C.** Love Love Me Do
   **D.** Many Waters

---

# HOW ABOUT THAT!

Contrary to popular opinion, *Away in a Manger,* was not written by Martin Luther—in fact, it's almost unknown in Germany!

---

6. The writer of "Be Thou My Vision" was what nationality?
   **A.** Irish
   **B.** Yiddish
   **C.** Scottish
   **D.** Hungarian

ANSWERS p. 305

7. "Jesus, I My Cross Have Taken" was written in which century?
   **A.** 8th
   **B.** 20th
   **C.** 19th
   **D.** 17th

---

**8. "The King of Love My Shepherd is" is based on what scripture?**
   **A.** Psalm 119
   **B.** Psalm 23
   **C.** Psalm 69
   **D.** Psalm 73

## MATCHING

1. O Love that Wilt Not Let Me Go

2. I Surrender All

3. Joy to the World

4. The Church's One Foundation

5. More Love to Thee

6. Jesus, I am Resting, Resting

7. Hark! the Herald Angels Sing

8. When All Thy Mercies, O My God

9. Take My Life and Let It Be

10. Jesus, I My Cross Have Taken

a. Charles Wesley

b. Isaac Watts

c. Elizabeth P. Prentiss

d. Henry F. Lyte

e. Jean Sophia Pigott

f. Joseph Addison

g. George Matheson

h. Samuel J. Stone

i. Judson W. Van De Venter

j. Frances R. Havergal

## FILL IN THE BLANKS

### Gregorian Chant

1. Gregorian chant was invented _____ a system of _____ writing had been invented.

2. Gregorian chant was invented because Charlemagne, king of the _____, wanted music in his kingdom to be sung like in _____.

3. Gregorian chant was named after a _____ of that period in order to give it greater _____.

4. _____ monks, in the _____ century, restored the melodies of the chants to their pre-seventeenth century forms.

ANSWERS p. 306

### WORD BANK

| | | |
|---|---|---|
| Solesmes | Gregorian | nineteenth |
| eighteenth | king | music | after |
| before | Franks | Rome | authority |
| | English | pope | |

## UNSCRAMBLE

1. Rome Vole
   ot Hete

2. Kaet Ym Eilf dan Elt ti Eb

3. Ganizam Ercag

4. Nitles Hingt

5. No Ronjads Roymst Skanb

6. Hertwi Anth Owns

7. Anthebe het Sorcs fo Sujes

8. Wrodan Tinahrics Resilosd

9. Yaaw ni a Gernam

10. Lelhalhaju, Thaw a Virsoa

ANSWERS
p. 306

## FILL IN THE BLANKS

### How Well Do You Know the Hymns?

1. _____ grace, how sweet the _____

   That saved a _____ like me!

   I _____ was lost, but now am found.

   Was _____ but now I _____!

---

When we've been _____ ten thousand years,

_____ shining as the _____,

We've \_\_\_\_ less days to \_\_\_\_\_ \_\_\_\_\_'s _____.

Than when we've first _____.

2. _____ as I am, without one _____

But that thy _____ was shed for me

And that thou _____ me come to thee

O Lamb of God, \_\_\_\_ _____! \_\_\_\_ _____!

*(ANSWERS p. 307)*

Just as I am, thy _____ unknown

Hath broken every _____ down

Now to be _____, yea _____ alone

O Lamb of God, \_\_\_\_ _____! \_\_\_\_ _____!

3. O for a thousand _____ to sing

My great Redeemer's _____

The _____ of my God and King

The _____ of his grace.

_____ him ye _____, his praise ye dumb

Your loosened tongues _____

Ye blind behold your Savior _____

And _____ ye lame for joy.

## TRUE OR FALSE

1. The word worship is used 223 times in the Bible.

2. "Worship" comes from Hebrew and Greek words that mean "Bow Down."

3. The hymn of worship that Mary sings in the New Testament when she discovers that she will bear the child Jesus is called *The Holy Confession.*

4. Worship in the Old Testament included making sacrifices.

5. David built the first Temple in which the Israelites worshiped God.

6. A worship service in the Old Testament Tabernacle included a person confessing his/her sins, making a sacrifice, sprinkling blood on the altar, and the priest pronouncing him/her forgiven.

7. Worship in the New Testament synagogue consisted of lessons, singing, eating, sermons, and prayers.

8. All hymns are males.

9. In the synagogue, the Torah was chanted from beginning to end every year.

10. Liturgies of the Christian church vary according to the country in which they are read.

## PUT THE FOLLOWING IN ORDER (when these hymns were written, from oldest to most recent)

Because He Lives

Be Thou My Vision

He Lives

O Perfect Love

O Sacred Head, Now Wounded

The Solid Rock

Tis So Sweet to Trust in Jesus

ANSWERS p. 309

Turn Your Eyes Upon Jesus

Joy to the World

I Need Thee Every Hour

## FILL IN THE BLANKS

### Christmas Carols!

1. Silent night, _____ night!

   All is calm, all is _____.

   Round _____ Virgin, Mother and Child.

   Holy _____ so tender and mild,

   Sleep in heavenly peace,

   Sleep in heavenly peace.

   Silent night, holy night!

   _____ quake at the sight.

   _____ stream from heaven afar

   Heavenly hosts sing _____,

   Christ the Savior is born!

   Christ the Savior is born.

   Silent night, holy night!

   _____ love's pure light.

   _____ beams from Thy holy face

ANSWERS
p. 309

With dawn of _____ grace,

Jesus Lord, at Thy birth.

Jesus Lord, at Thy birth.

2.  O _____, all ye faithful,

Joyful and _____,

O come ye, O come ye to _____;

Come and _____ Him,

Born the King of _____;

O come, let us adore Him,

O come, let us adore Him,

O come, let us adore Him,

Christ, the Lord.

Sing, _____ of angels,

Sing in _____,

O sing all ye _____ of heaven above;

Glory to God,

All glory in the highest;

Yea, Lord we _____ thee,

Born this _____ morning,

Jesus, to thee be all _____ given;

_____ of the Father,

Now in flesh appearing;

**3.** O holy night! The _____ are brightly shining

It is the _____ of the dear Savior's birth!

_____ lay the world in sin and error pining

Till he appear'd and the soul felt its _____.

A _____ of hope the weary world rejoices

For _____ breaks a new and glorious morn!

Fall on your _____

Oh hear the _____ voices

Oh night _____

Oh night when Christ was born

Oh night divine

Oh night divine

Led by the light of Faith _____ beaming

With _____ hearts by His cradle we stand

So led by light of a _____ sweetly gleaming

Here come the wise men from _____ land

The King of Kings lay _____ in lowly manger

In all our _____ born to be our friend

_____ He taught us to love one another

His _____ is love and His gospel is peace

_____ shall He break for the slave is our brother

And in His name all _____ shall cease

Sweet _____ of joy in grateful chorus raise we,

Let all within us _____ His holy name.

4. Bring a torch, _____, Isabella

    ANSWERS
    p. 310

    Bring a torch, to the _____ run!

    It is Jesus good _____ of the village;

    Christ is born and _____ calling;

    Ah! ah! _____ is the mother

    Ah! ah! beautiful is her _____!

    It is wrong when the _____ is sleeping

    It is wrong to _____ so loud;

    Silence, all, as you gather around.

    Lest your noise should waken Jesus.

    Hush! hush! see how _____ he sleeps!

# Top Ten Rejected Christmas Carols

10. We Wish You a Hairy Christmas

9. Got Arrested, You Merry Gentlemen?

8. Hark, Harold the Angel Sneezes!

7. I Saw Three Ships Sink

6. I Might Be Home for Christmas

5. Santa Claus Is Coming to Get Me

4. The Day After Christmas

3. Rudolph, the Red-nosed Chandelier

2. We Three Kings Disoriented Are

1. O Come All Ye Hangnails!

Hasten now, good _____ of the village;

Hasten now the Christ Child to _____.

You will find him _____ in the manger;

_____ come and whisper softly,

Hush! hush! _____ now he sleeps.

Softly to the little _____.

Softly in a _____ come;

Look and see how _____ is Jesus

how he is white, his cheeks are _____!

Hush! hush! see how the _____ is sleeping;

Hush! hush! see how he _____ in his dreams.

# HOW ABOUT THAT!

The tune to *A Mighty Fortress* was taken from a popular bar song during Martin Luther's life.

5. Good Christian men, _____

   With heart and _____ and voice;

   Give ye _____ to what we say;

   News! News! Jesus _____ is born today!

_____ and ass before him bow, he is in the manger now;

Christ is born today! Christ is born today!

Good _____ men, rejoice,

With _____ and soul and voice;

Now ye hear of endless _____,

Jesus Christ was _____ for this!

He has _____ the heav'nly door

And man is blessed evermore.

Christ was born for _____! Christ was born for _____!

_____ Christian men, rejoice,

With heart and soul and _____;

Now ye _____ not fear the grave;

Jesus Christ is born to _____.

_____ you one and calls you all,

To gain His everlasting _____.

Christ was born to save! Christ was born to save!

---

If you want to know when Charles Wesley wrote his first song, you'll have to ask hymn!

---

# ANSWERS TO:
# WORSHIP

## FILL IN THE BLANKS

| # | ANSWER |
|---|--------|
| 1. | hymn singing |
| 2. | blessings, creatures, above all, Father, Son, Ghost |
| 3. | Gloria Patri |
| 4. | Gloria in Excelsis |

## MULTIPLE CHOICE

| # | ANSWER |
|---|--------|
| 1. | b |
| 2. | c |
| 3. | c |
| 4. | a |
| 5. | b |
| 6. | a |
| 7. | c |
| 8. | b |

## MATCHING

| # | ANSWER |
|---|--------|
| 1. | g |
| 2. | i |
| 3. | b |
| 4. | h |
| 5. | c |
| 6. | e |
| 7. | a |
| 8. | f |
| 9. | j |
| 10. | d |

## FILL IN THE BLANKS

| # | ANSWER |
|---|--------|
| 1. | before, music |
| 2. | Franks, Rome |
| 3. | Pope, authority |
| 4. | Solesmes, nineteenth |

## UNSCRAMBLE

| # | ANSWER |
|---|--------|
| 1. | More Love to Thee |
| 2. | Take My Life and Let It Be |

| # | ANSWER |
|---|--------|
| 3. | Amazing Grace |
| 4. | Silent Night |
| 5. | On Jordan's Stormy Banks |
| 6. | Whiter Than Snow |
| 7. | Beneath the Cross of Jesus |
| 8. | Onward, Christian Soldiers |
| 9. | Away in a Manger |
| 10. | Hallelujah, What a Savior |

## FILL IN THE BLANKS

| # | ANSWER |
|---|--------|
| 1. | Amazing, sound |
| | wretch |
| | once |
| | blind, see |
| | |
| | there |
| | bright, sun |
| | no, sing, God, praise |
| | begun |
| 2. | Just, plea |
| | blood |
| | bidst |
| | I come, I come |
| | love |
| | barrier |

## FILL IN THE
## BLANKS—cont'd

| # | ANSWER |
|---|--------|
| | thine, thine |
| | I come, I come |
| 3. | tongues |
| | praise |
| | glories |
| | triumphs |
| | hear, deaf |
| | employ |
| | come |
| | leap |

## TRUE OR
## FALSE

| # | ANSWER | REFERENCE |
|---|--------|-----------|
| 1. | False | each translation is different |
| 2. | True | |
| 3. | False | *Magnificat* |
| 4. | True | |
| 5. | False | Solomon built the Temple |
| 6. | True | |
| 7. | False | no eating |
| 8. | False! | |
| 9. | True | |
| 10. | True | |

## PUT THE FOLLOWING IN ORDER

| # ANSWER | DATE |
|---|---|
| 1. Be Thou My Vision | 8th c. |
| 2. O Sacred Head, Now Wounded | 12th c. |
| 3. Joy to the World | 1719 |
| 4. The Solid Rock | 1834 |
| 5. I Need Thee Every Hour | 1872 |
| 6. Tis So Sweet to Trust in Jesus | 1879 |
| 7. O Perfect Love | 1883 |
| 8. Turn Your Eyes Upon Jesus | 1918 |
| 9. He Lives | 1933 |
| 10. Because He Lives | 1960s |

## FILL IN THE BLANKS

| # ANSWER |
|---|
| 1. holy, bright, yon, infant<br>shepherds, glories, alleluia<br>Son of God, radiant, redeeming |
| 2. come, triumphant, Bethlehem, behold, Angels<br>choirs, exultation, citizens<br>greet, happy, glory, Word |

| # | ANSWER |
|---|--------|

3. stars, night, long, worth, thrill, yonder
   knees, angel, divine
   serenely, glowing, star, Orient, thus, trials
   truly, law, chains, oppression, hymns, praise

4. Jeanette, cradle, folks, Mary
   beautiful, son, Child
   talk, fast, folk, see, asleep, quietly, peacefully
   stable, moment, charming, rosey, child, smiling

5. rejoice, soul, heed, Christ, ox
   Christian, heart, bliss, born, op'ed, this, this
   Good, voice, need, save, calls, hall